From the Heart

From the Heart

Stories of Hope, Passion, and Purpose

ROBERT CHARLES PAYNE

PELICAN PUBLISHING COMPANY

Gretna 2012

*The word "Pelican" and the depiction of a pelican are
trademarks of Pelican Publishing Company, Inc., and are
registered in the U.S. Patent and Trademark Office.*

ISBN 9781589809710
E-book ISBN 9781455615483

Printed in the United States of America
Published by Pelican Publishing Company, Inc.
1000 Burmaster Street, Gretna, Louisiana 70053

To my grandchildren,
Elizabeth Grace, Gracen Hope, Kendall Beck,
Addelyn Faith, and Hutson Beck

Contents

Acknowledgments

I would like to thank Mrs. Camille Adair for reading and editing the manuscript. I want to thank my daughter Laurie Devone Payne for typing the entire book, making corrections, and arranging the manuscript in its final form. I would also like to thank my daughter for her constant support. I offer my appreciation to those at Pelican Publishing for their encouragement and their patience.

Introduction

This book is the result of many people who encouraged me to write a book that related to the articles that I have written for our Sunday school class and the weekly columns that I have written for the *Ouachita Citizen*. I was getting so many compliments that I knew my writing was touching a personal chord. Thus, *From the Heart* was birthed.

This book is an accumulation of accounts from people's lives and the relationships that are formed through similar life lessons. It is a collection of sketches that can be read in one sitting or enjoyed over a period of time. No matter in which manner they are read, they can guide you on a passage that leads to an emotional ride of encouragement, pain, ecstasy, disappointment, victory, or defeat; but in the end, the reader experiences the joy of overcoming. Through lessons of overcoming, the reader learns to identify with the stories and the life lessons that are revealed.

Life is a universal barometer. Some of the stories are short biographical portrayals, while others are autobiographical in nature. Whether the stories are biographical or autobiographical, the interaction that is created with the reader's life conveys a message that life is about overcoming.

Some associations might be made by the reader because he has had a life of successful overcoming. If the reader is battling with life, he knows through the associations that he has made with certain events that he, too, can overcome.

Each story enfolds around the reader's own wants and desires, thus arousing the deep psychological drama that plays out in the reader's own life. The excitement of the awakened passion encourages the reader to accelerate his own ideas of expectations. This book can make you feel. Each story has a motive. And that motive is to encourage and inspire the reader. If I could sum up the theme of this book in one sentence, it would be for the reader to reach for the stars and never give up.

Regaining a Passion for Life

Older people and, God forbid, even younger people lose their passion for living. Many people ask, "How can I regain my passion?"

I think the best answer for that question is to get a mission that you are excited about. Joseph of the Bible had a passion for his dream. When he shared his dream with his own family, jealousy grew from sibling rivalries. Sometimes it is best to not share your dreams with others. Believe it or not, some people don't want your dreams to come true.

Joseph never allowed the adversity that continually came into his life to discourage him. He never lost his passion for living nor for achieving the dream that he had had since he was a young boy, even though his brothers threw him into a pit and later sold him into slavery. Even though Joseph was falsely accused by his boss's wife of trying to sexually molest her, he was thrown into prison. Even though Joseph successfully interpreted the dreams of two other prisoners that allowed their release from prison, even though they forgot their promise to Joseph to remember him so he might be released from prison as well, even though he languished in jail for two more years, he never gave up on his dreams. He had every reason to become bitter, but bitterness and resentment were never a part of Joseph's psyche. He continued to keep his passion for living, for he knew that somehow he would be given the opportunity to realize his childhood dreams.

After fourteen years of continuous trials, the opportunity that would catapult him into a position that would finally bring success to his lifelong dreams appeared. He interpreted Pharaoh's dreams and, because of his successful interpretations, was released from prison. Joseph became the second most powerful man in Egypt.

Joseph never allowed himself to focus on the hardships and injustices that he faced for fourteen years. Instead, he kept his eyes on the dream he desired so strongly that his passion for reaching it never died. He could have quit at any time during the journey, especially since it looked as if he would forever be blocked by difficulty and affliction. However, he knew that if he would keep hanging on, no matter what, then one day he would see his dreams come true. His passion and beliefs brought manifestation to the images that he had held in his mind ever since he was a boy.

I can hear the older person saying, "Robert Charles, I missed it. I cannot reach the dreams of my life. What can I do now? It is too late." You may not know it, but so many of us have missed it. I missed it. But what can we do when we think that it is too late? First of all, it is never too late. We can always dream again. Maybe they are not the same youthful dreams that we once had but new dreams for a new time. Maybe you are like me. I am over sixty years of age. What can an older person do? We think that we are too old. The world has convinced us that we are too old. No! Never!

Remember this: no one can keep you from dreaming. Discover what gives you a new passion and start living again. It is never too late.

For Better or for Worse

Vows—words of commitment and promise. On March 21, 2001, I was strongly reminded of my marriage vows: "For richer or poorer, for better or worse, in sickness and in health." When I saw my wife lying there on that hospital bed, the reality of my marriage vows became very factual. Only moments before, Dr. William Ferguson had told me that Donna, my wife, had breast cancer. I asked him if she knew it yet, and he said that she did not. I asked him if I could go with him when he told her.

I remember walking through the door and seeing her lying on that bed. Tears began to well up in my eyes. I knew that, at that moment, she did not know that she had cancer but that, within the next thirty seconds, our lives would radically change.

As Dr. Ferguson, one of the most compassionate doctors that you will ever meet, told Donna that she had cancer, I took hold of her hand. Only those who have experienced this moment know what I am talking about when I say I took hold of her hand. I noticed a big tear roll down her cheek. She told me that she did not know if she could go through with this or not.

She had watched as my mother had gone through an agonizing last six months of life battling lung cancer. She knew from firsthand experience about chemo, radiation, and the progressive onslaught of cancer. I reassured her that we were going to make it through this. Cancer is a "we" thing, not an "I" thing.

From the moment that I had stood in the door and seen Donna on that hospital bed, all I could think about was our marriage vows. And the words "in sickness and in health" were my dominating thoughts. I recalled saying them at our wedding, but I was reminded of the actual commitment: "In sickness and in health, in sickness and in health, in sickness and in health." I wanted to protect her. Trade places with her. I wanted it to go away.

I thought about some of the rough times in our marriage. There had been words that were said that should not have been said. The anger that we felt when we had disagreements could have caused our marriage to fall apart. But at that moment, I knew why we had been able to survive those trying times.

Every negative event that had happened in our marriage disappeared instantly.

Now I was being guided by a love for Donna that completely engulfed all of my emotions. I knew that I needed to love Donna as strongly as I ever had—not because I needed to, but because I wanted to. I wanted her to get well, and I knew that I was going to do whatever it took to get her well. Problems were no longer important. Worldly matters were no longer important. Getting her well was all that mattered.

I have watched as so many members of the Payne family died from cancer, including my own mom and dad. Now the challenge of this ugly illness was staring Donna and me squarely in the face. As I left the recovery room that day, those marriage vows that Donna and I had shared thirty-three years ago became living words, words that drove me to do whatever it took to get my bride completely free of cancer.

When cancer strikes a spouse, the "I do" becomes "we do." Yes, Donna and I have discovered there is a big difference between spoken words and living words.

Giving Life Your
Best Shot Is All That's Required

Have you ever felt saddened by an event in your life? How did you respond? I lost my father when I was in the eighth grade. This tragedy caused years of questioning and years of adjustments.

My father had been a well-respected coach, and I was used to having a lot of attention because I was one of Coach Payne's boys. During those years when I kept questioning, I would look for a church at night in which I could go pray. Even back in the '60s, most churches locked their doors, but there was one church next to my church that always left their doors unlocked. They also left some lights dimly lit, which gave the sanctuary a calm presence. Sometimes I would sit for several hours with thoughts of "why?" running through my mind. There were times when I just sat there with tears rolling down my cheeks. I wanted answers. It was hard growing up without a father during my teenage years. I missed him. I needed him.

Where do you go when you are saddened or disturbed by life's challenges, whether it is from your marriage, your job, your children, your relationships, or your finances? There are two places that I visit that have always brought me peace. One place is the church. The other is a stadium or football field.

I was so grateful for many years because I could go to the sanctuary of the Pentecostal Church when it was on Montgomery Street in West Monroe, Louisiana. I would walk into the slightly lit auditorium and find a place to sit, usually on the second or third row toward the front. Directly above the baptistery was a big cross that was a reminder of why I was there.

Most of the time, I would sit quietly and listen. There were times when others were scattered throughout the sanctuary voicing their prayers. One day, there was a lady seated in the back. I had never heard such sincere prayers in all my life, and I almost felt guilty because I could hear her praying. I can remember saying, "Lord, is it all right if I just ditto everything that she prays?" I knew that I could not improve upon her straight talk with God.

There have been times since I left as the head football coach at West Monroe High School twenty-eight years ago that I have sat in Rebel Stadium at night. I looked at the stadium lights, standing there like big skeletons looking over the battle ground for so many gridiron wars. I tried to make sense out of the journey of the Payne family, asking those "what if" questions that never do a bit of good. I usually came to terms with the "whys" before my session in Rebel Stadium was over. The answers were highly influenced by my mother's philosophy of always counting your blessings.

I learned one thing as I looked heavenward so many times from that stadium. It is the journey that each of us travel that is so important. It is the people that we have met, the places that we have been, and all the events that have taken place. Schools, graduations, marriages, divorces, successes, failings, hospitals, births, deaths, family, holidays, sports events, pageants, recitals, hunting and fishing trips, getting your driver's license, dating, parties, visiting, reunions, friends, those special pets—these are the footprints that mark the paths of our journey.

As we enter the final chapters of life, and when all is said and done, if we have given it our best shot, that is all that is required.

Those Early Childhood Dreams

When I was a little boy, one of my dreams was to become the president of the United States. I am sure that many children dream of becoming president and living in that big White House. We have so many dreams when we are young. Our imaginations have not been conditioned or limited. Our minds soar with the eagles.

I thought that being a preacher might be interesting. I remember thinking that the preacher had a good job. He worked only one day, and that was just for an hour. I always wondered what he did for the rest of the week.

My number one dream as a young boy was to play professional sports—all of them. When we are young, our imaginations can take us anywhere that we want to go. We can dream of becoming anybody we want to be. We never think about impossibilities.

How many of us have been a cowboy or an Indian at one point in our lives? When I was little, playing cowboys and Indians was one of our favorite pastimes. We would all go to the movies on Saturday mornings to watch the "shoot-em ups" at the Bailey Theater in Tallulah, Louisiana.

> *"If we give a child the right keys at the right time, he can unlock his own potential."*
>
> Robert Charles Payne

The movies were called picture shows back then. Roy Rogers, Gene Autry, Lash LaRue, Tom Mix, the Lone Ranger and Tonto—these were long before Clint Eastwood. Oh, yes, before you say something smart, we did have talking

21

movies. When the picture show ended, we would all go home to play cowboys and Indians.

What is it that causes us to lose sight of our early childhood dreams and all the imagination that goes with childhood? How many times have you heard young people comment that they did not know what they wanted to do with their lives? Older folks are not immune to this doubt either. What would it have taken to have jump-started us when we were young so that we could become focused on that which makes us feel passionate about living?

More time should be spent in our educational curriculum to help students discover their dreams. I would love to see the college professor telling the teacher aspirants to be more cognizant of the student's passion light when it comes on and to be trained to recognize the moment when that spark gives birth to the giant within.

It is at that moment that the teacher should know that it is time to begin feeding the giant. Chances are, if the teacher does not recognize the glowing embers of desire waiting to be fanned to ignite the substance of dreams, the child could join the ranks of the mediocre who go through life wandering aimlessly in the wilderness for the next forty years. Teacher, don't miss that moment.

Don't get me wrong! I have always been a big believer in reading, writing, and arithmetic; but sandwiched somewhere in between all these courses, there should be some courses that are only for the development of the students' dreams.

Some of the brightest and most imaginative students never fit into our box system, where everyone does and learns the same thing because that is the way it has always been done. Teachers should be Dream Builders and become guides for the young who have new ideas in their brains.

There is only a slight difference between a giant and an ant. There is only a small difference between the common and the uncommon. God's marvels are invisible to the ordinary man; but the ordinary man becomes extraordinary, the common becomes uncommon, and the ant becomes the giant when their visions begin to exceed their grasps.

NASCAR in Crowville

You would have thought that we were training to become NASCAR drivers as we learned to drive on the back roads near Crowville, Louisiana. Well, we thought we were race car drivers. The track stretched from my Granddaddy Payne's house all the way to Uncle Alton's and Uncle Rufus's houses on Bayou Macon some five miles away. One of us would drive from Granddaddy Payne's to our uncles' houses, and then another person would drive on the way back.

Learning to drive on these country gravel roads prepared my brother Devone, several cousins, Don Payne, Fabian Geisman, and me for the big day to which every teenager looks forward—the day that we would take the driving test for our driver's license. We were already advanced students by the time this important event took place.

We used two different cars most of the time—Granddaddy's old straight stick Dodge and Aunt Doxie's push-button Dodge. They were bought at Lanier Motor Company in Winnsboro, Louisiana. Aunt Doxie's car was cool. We didn't have to worry about a thing; we just had to push the button.

Now the straight shift was another story. After killing the engine many times from all the jerking and jumping because we did not know exactly when to release the clutch, we would finally get the hang of it. It was like filming a scene in the movies: "Take one . . . take two . . . take three." The cycle went on and on until we finally got the car past the jerking and jumping stage. Then we would get the car all leveled out and running smoothly down those graveled roads. We all would have rather driven the straight stick because of the shifts between gears. I am not sure what we did to Granddaddy Payne's car, because that second gear was great for potential race car drivers. Before that last shift into high gear, we could get that motor roaring. By that time, we had that car moving, throwing rocks all over the road and kicking up enough dust so that it looked like a cattle drive was on the way. We knew that we were ready for NASCAR because we never ran into a ditch or had any kind of wreck.

I can only imagine what the cost of our self-taught driver's training course would be today with the price of gasoline as high as it is compared to the price of gasoline in the early fifties. I think it was 28.9 cents a gallon for regular. Today's prices would have put an end to our driver's training course in Crowville.

All of us had graduated from driving a tractor to driving a car or truck except for my brother and me. We did not have any tractors at our house in the city. Devone and I did not get much agricultural training in Monroe, Louisiana. There were not many members of the FFA at Neville High School.

Since my cousins were all reared on a farm, they were well-trained by the time they came of age to drive a car, which was anywhere from eight to ten years old if you lived in Crowville. None of us became Richard Petty, but Devone and I did have one cousin, Donald Payne, who learned to drive his vehicle at several hundred miles an hour. In fact, he drove his vehicle so fast that it would finally leave the ground. Donald became a crop duster.

All of the Payne family learned to drive on the back roads around Crowville. Our country driver's courses must have been a success because we have all survived over fifty years of driving.

Queenie Was a Redbone Hound

Queenie was her name. She was a redbone hound who belonged to my Uncle Rufus. We would use Queenie for coon hunting at night and squirrel hunting by day.

A lot of times when we went to visit Grandmother and Granddaddy Payne for a few nights, we would go coon hunting out in front of their house—Daddy, Uncle Rufus, Devone, my cousins Don and Fabian and Donald, and I. Maybe another uncle would come along. We did not hunt too long because everyone went to bed fairly early, but we went long enough to enjoy the hunt and listen to the howls of Queenie when she treed a coon.

Then there were days that we would take Queenie with us to the woods around Crowville. This land covered about two thousand acres, and it was owned by Mr. Collier, who lived in Crowville. I can remember driving up to a dirt road that stopped at the edge of the woods. Since we did not have a jeep or tractor, we parked our car and walked into the woods to squirrel hunt. Daddy usually brought his 30-30 rifle just in case that whitetail jumped out in front of us. Devone and I would have our 410 JC Higgins bolt-action shotguns that were ordered right out of the Sears and Roebuck catalogue.

After years of hunting with dogs, I never quite mastered still hunting. We would both sit down and wait for Queenie to tree, or we would walk very slowly in the direction that Queenie was headed. It would not be long before we would hear Queenie's deep base howl, signaling that she had treed a squirrel.

Queenie would catch several squirrels on the ground, and they would head for one of those huge oak trees. However, Queenie was usually at the base of the tree, circling around it with her head up and eyes looking for the hunkered down critters. Sometimes we could not get them to move, and so we would start throwing sticks up into the tree, an action which would sometimes spook the squirrels into running either further up the tree or back down it toward the ground. Daddy had always trained us to be careful when the squirrels headed back down. Often the squirrels would hit the ground running and head toward another tree. If they made it to a tree with a hole or nest, it would usually take some tricks to get them out again.

Walking for several miles through the woods was an outdoor adventure. There was nothing more beautiful than a hardwood bottom with a slough that might run several hundred yards and be full of wood ducks and mallards. Sometimes we did get eight or ten squirrels, and maybe a duck or two, along with that rabbit that we jumped as we walked through the woods. We weren't duck hunters, but these sloughs were too inviting not to take a shot when they appeared. The memory of the sounds of the mallards quacking and the wood ducks squealing still awakens that little hunter in me.

I remember so many of these hunts, but what I remember most is that God created the woods with all the colors, the seasons, the cold weather, the ice on the water, and the different wildlife. We would even hear the scream of a panther, and although we never saw one, we did see a few bobcats and foxes. Much of the woods are gone now, but mankind can never cut away the memories of hunting with our daddy and ole' Queenie.

Still Better to Keep It Simple

A while back, I wrote a column about the KISS method. KISS is an acronym for "Keep It Simple, Stupid." I have found that it is always better to keep it simple, and I have several stories to share today that will give accounts for simplicity.

The first story comes from the former head football coach of Ruston High School. When Coach "Chick" Childress was hired at Ruston, the football program had fallen on hard times. He had inherited a program that was in disarray, and not many people were participating in other extracurricular activities either. Even the band was small.

Ruston was opening the season against the Southwood Cowboys from Shreveport. At that time, Southwood had an outstanding program. Before the game began,

> "Character is what we do when we are alone."
>
> Robert Charles Payne

Childress was standing outside the dressing room to see what kind of crowd that they might have for their home opener. About that time, the Southwood band came marching in. He said he did not think they would ever get to the end. Band members kept coming and coming.

Childress quickly moved to the back of the stadium where the Ruston band, about half the size of the Southwood band, was gathered. They were about to make their entrance. Childress drew the Ruston band director off to the side.

"I want you to do something for me. When your band begins marching in, make sure that the band members that come in first do not sit down. Have them keep marching, go around the back of the stadium, and have them come in again. I think if everyone does it twice before anyone sits down, it might make them believe that we have a much larger band."

Now that is one way to grow a band.

Another story involves a college coach from Vanderbilt University. He was looking at one of Ruston's defensive backs. The coach from Vanderbilt asked Childress what the defensive back's time was in the 40-yard dash. Childress said he did not have a clue. The Vanderbilt coach was startled by his answer.

"Coach, you mean you don't know his 40-yard dash time?" Childress answered again, "No."

"Coach, do you time your players in the 40-yard dash?" Childress said matter of factly, "No, I don't. Why should I?"

Childress said the coach looked puzzled, and he could tell the coach was struggling with the answer; but the coach finally said, "I don't know."

The next story involves John Curtis High School. John Curtis, Jr., the head football coach, was sharing this story with his fellow coaches at a clinic. He said that his team had run all over their opponents. John Curtis runs the veer offense, and the dive play is the first option in the veer. Their opponents had not been able to stop the simple dive play. They ran the same play all night because the opponent had not stopped that one simple play yet. He said that he had called time out to talk to his quarterback.

When the quarterback got to the sidelines, Curtis asked him, "Son, do you think that we can get outside on our pitch play?"

To which the quarterback answered, "Sure, coach. But why?"

When I was coaching a little boy's football team, I saw the following incident happen during one of our games.

It was first and ten for our opponents. Their little quarterback hollered over to his coach on the sidelines, "What do you want me to run?"

"I don't care. Run anything that you want."

He punted.

Small-Town Experiences—Priceless

I loved living in Tallulah, Louisiana. Most of our experiences included the whole family. At that time, there were only two of us boys, my older brother, Devone Jr., and me. When I think back on those times, I think of the simplicity of life. Maybe it was because I was only a child and did not know there were any problems. Mother and Daddy never discussed problems within our hearing range. We were never aware that we did not have much money. So as far as my brother and I knew, everything was always great.

What we did for entertainment, as the advertisement says on television, was priceless. I can remember going to the Coca-Cola bottling plant there in Tallulah. The manager of the plant was a close friend of our family, and his wife had been a cheerleader with my mother at Louisiana College. Sometimes we could go into the plant and watch the production of the Coca-Colas. One empty bottle after another was lined up on the conveyer belt and being filled with Coca-Cola, and then the tops would seal each drink. The final products would be fitted into each wooden case that was then loaded onto the trucks for delivery. I never tired of watching the process.

I don't believe I enjoyed anything any better than our Sunday afternoon rides throughout the countryside. I know we must have traveled every road in Madison Parish and a few in the Franklin and Tensas Parishes. Daddy loved to choose the roads less traveled.

Deer were plentiful in the '40s and '50s. We were always seeing deer roaming in the fields or crossing the road in front of the car. We would ride on the Mississippi River levee as far as the gates would allow. It was as if we were riding through a safari. Many times, there were so many deer in the pastures along the levee that we would first think they were a herd of cattle. Sometimes we could get on the levee north of Tallulah and go as far as St. Joseph. Several times a year, we would include a picnic by one of the bar pits between the levee and the Mississippi River.

Sometimes we rode the back roads at night. It was not unusual to see over a hundred deer in one field. Many times when we came home from Crowville after visiting with Grandmother and Granddaddy Payne, we would take the old gravel road that ran along the Boeuf and Tensas Rivers and exited south of Tallulah on the Newellton Highway.

This back road trip took us through the Sharkey Hunting Club, one of the best hunting clubs in the area. I saw barrels in trees along the Tensas River that were used as tree stands. Even though I had never hunted out of a tree stand, I would have liked being in one early in the morning when it was still dark. I would feel safe from all those monsters that I heard walking through the woods before daybreak.

There is one thing that neighbors did back then, and that was visit. Several of the families would get together every Wednesday night after prayer meeting. Parents visited. Kids played outside. There was nothing fancy or expensive. But the experiences in Tallulah were priceless.

Rudolph, the Red-Nosed Reindeer

Have you ever felt rejected and ostracized by your peers? Were you ever taunted by your school mates for being different? Maybe you were very shy. Maybe you were considered a "small fry." Were you ever considered ugly? Maybe you were an overweight child. Were you ever insulted because of your weight? Were you skinny and the kids called you beanpole? What about your eyesight? Were you ever called four-eyes? Were you ever awkward and kids called you clumsy? In other words, was something about you considered an abnormality by others around you?

There are so many things that can happen to us as we go through life. Some unkind comments that were made about us when we were young have been part of our psyche since the day that we heard them. Some of us never recover and allow these stinging darts to our hearts influence how we feel about ourselves. Our self-esteem suffers and we are never able to heal from these psychological wounds. Yes, there are some of us who can see the glass as half-filled and not half-empty. They are able to convert the negative experiences of life into stepping stones instead of stumbling blocks. Into which category do you fall?

One of the biggest failures for most of his life was Abraham Lincoln. He was not handsome. He was very awkward looking. He was elected only once to Congress over a twenty-four-year period. He was defeated nine out of eleven times for political office. His life was filled with so much heartache and pain, yet he transformed the negatives of his life into the strong qualities that are required of leadership.

34

His transformation led him to not just any leadership position, but the leadership that was required of the president of the United States to lead this country through the most tragic time in its history—the Civil War.

Now what in the world do Abraham Lincoln and Rudolph, the red-nosed reindeer, have in common? Much more than we may think. As I was driving down the road the other day, I was enjoying the Christmas music on the radio and singing every word of each song. Then, as I caught myself singing about Rudolph, the red-nosed reindeer, I realized what a great teaching lesson this song would make for all the children, and even the adults, who have felt rejected and ostracized by others.

Here was a little reindeer who suffered from being different. His nose was not like those of the other reindeer. It was red and it even glowed. The other reindeer said that Rudolph was abnormal. They laughed at him, called him names, and would not even let him play any of their games. Then one Christmas Eve when the weather was foggy, Santa Claus realized that Rudolph had what it took to be a leader. He was different, and because he was different, he was the only reindeer that could lead the way to deliver all the presents to all the boys and girls. When the other reindeer recognized that Rudolph was going to become their leader, they all lined up behind him.

So when you hear this amazing story in song about Rudolph, the red-nosed reindeer, be reminded that he became the leader because he was different. Now you know why Abraham Lincoln and Rudolph, the red-nosed reindeer, have so much in common.

The Circle of Influence

If I could choose ten people to teach me about life, who would they be? My mother and father, Jesus Christ, Abraham Lincoln, Bill Gates, Leonardo da Vinci, Oprah Winfrey, Og Mandino, Walter Russell, and Joseph of the Bible's Old Testament.

I would want my mother and father to be included because I came from them and was greatly influenced by them psychologically, spiritually, and socially. They both had characteristics that I admire. Mother was intelligent, disciplined, strong, unselfish, devoted to her family, and encouraging. My daddy was a leader, and he taught boys how to become men. His coaching went far beyond the football field. He was humble, and he cared deeply for those less fortunate.

Jesus Christ would also be a choice. I would like to observe the human side of Him. I want to learn the power of service to mankind. I want to observe the principle of faith and how it influences decisions.

President Lincoln had many qualities that I would like to incorporate into my own character. He could have been considered a failure up to a certain point in his life, but his overcoming of adversity prepared him for the greatest and most demanding role of leadership in the history of our country. When I think of Lincoln, I think of his capacity for perseverance.

I included Bill Gates because of his ability to take an idea and change the world with it. I would like for him to tell me about the amount of pressure that accompanies his wealth, which is greater than that of some countries. I want him to speak about the transformation from his business in a garage to one that grew into one of the most influential companies in the history of mankind. I would like to hear him tell how one develops the ability to handle a few bucks to managing billions of dollars. I would like to hear him describe the methods that he uses to stay focused.

> *"Only those who see the invisible can do the impossible."*
> *The Holy Bible*

Lately, we have heard a lot about Leonardo da Vinci. He was 500 years ahead of his time. I want him to communicate to me how one man can be so talented in so many areas.

I would ask Oprah to talk about her life before she became one of the most powerful people in the world. She had so much against her; she was sexually abused and knew racism and poverty. She should have failed. She should have been so psychologically damaged by the time she was a teenager that there was no way that she could be successful. However, she had a burning desire to achieve, and she believed in her dreams. I would like for her to convey to me who or what built that fire of desire in her.

Og Mandino is my inspiration as a writer. What were his motives that drove him to write such encouraging stories? What changed him from a suicidal, alcoholic failure to one of the most successful writers ever?

Walter Russell is probably a modern day da Vinci. He was self-educated. He never had a formal education. I want him to address how he tapped into this universal knowledge that is available to us all but to which only a few of us make the connection.

And lastly, I would ask Joseph about his ability to forgive so many that hurt him so badly. How did he keep his mind on his vision while so many Job-like experiences enveloped him?

Wow! What a wonderfully exciting time it would be to sit among these men and women. Is it possible for our imagination to create a circle of mentors who could give us the keys that unlock the doors to all possibilities?

When Your Light Goes Out

When your light goes out, the bugs go away.

Every athlete, politician, actor, actress, beauty queen, coach, person in a leadership position, preacher, or anyone who has been in a position of influence or in a vocation that brings notoriety, understands the meaning of these words.

After my father died when I was thirteen, I learned the meaning of these words. Since he was a successful football coach, his popularity brought us much attention. When he died, the crowds fell off. Many people quit coming around.

Another good example is the time when my wife and I had gotten up early to go eat a birthday breakfast before I went to work. When we had settled into our booth, we noticed a long-time politician sitting at the other end of the little restaurant. He had been a high-ranking politician for many, many years, but he had been defeated in the last election. He was alone and no one was coming over to shake his hand or trying to get his attention as they would have if he had still been in office. He sat there unnoticed. I felt a tinge of sadness for him. I did not feel sorry for the politician, but I did feel sorry for the man.

I am sure that this was a first-time learning experience for this man who had met with presidents, traveled the world, and visited world leaders. He was accustomed to all the attention that men and women of influential positions receive but who are not prepared to face the world of the unrecognized.

I have heard several people who had been in important positions remark about their retirements. They said, "It has been nice, but I miss the power." I think of the tremendous problem that Elvis Presley had when dealing with his light becoming dimmer. When athletes are faced with the reality that they are no longer important, or even recognizable, their lives become a challenge that they have never known before.

Have you ever been around athletes who have lost some of their former light and all they want to talk about is the old days? They want to talk about all the games, the great runs, the big tackle, and the great catch. Now, I don't want you to think that I think it is wrong to stand around and talk about some good times, but what I am referring to is the person who wants to talk about

> "Success . . . seems to be connected with action. Successful people keep moving. They make mistakes, but they don't quit."
> Conrad Hilton

the same games, runs, and tackles every time you get together. I have witnessed coaches who have known the limelight because of the successes of their teams and the glamour and adoration that those successes brought them become bitter after they retire because they were no longer appreciated.

The greatest shock to many is the realization that it was what you were—not who you were—that attracted people to you. It is not that they liked you so much or were drawn to you by your electric personality, but they wanted to be part of your importance and influence. I can remember the welcome that I received when I started my insurance career compared to my last days as an agent. When I began, everybody came by. Everybody called. I was "the man." When I retired, my phone remained very quiet. My light had gone out.

There are two things of which you can be assured: "The size of your funeral will be determined by the weather," and "When your light goes out, the bugs go away."

What's on Your Mind

Has anyone ever caught you staring off into space and asked, "What's on your mind?" This question came to mind one day as I was riding in my car. I knew that there was more to this question than meets the eye—a lot more. We probably need to be asking ourselves this question more frequently, because what we think about does influence the way we live.

The tendency to hold a negative attitude in our thought process leads to a negative environment. The constant expression of negative remarks can create an environment that is harmful and detrimental. We have a tendency to draw to ourselves what we speak and think about. Listen to some of the comments that we make:

"If it were not for bad luck, I would not have any luck at all."

"When it rains, it pours."

"It's just my luck."

"When you are hot, you are hot. When you are not, you're not."

"If anything bad is going to happen, it will probably happen to me."

"Everyone is against me."

"If I had his money, good things would happen to me too."

The next time that you are in a bad mood, stop and reflect. What have you been thinking lately? What have you been reading lately? What have you been listening to lately? What have you been watching lately? You will have your answer.

Do you remember the rich uncle in the old Donald Duck comic books? Donald Duck's rich uncle seemed to always have the best of luck, but if you looked closely at each cartoon, you would see that Donald Duck's uncle always thought that good things were going to happen to him. His expectant attitude always attracted good things. In his case, it was money.

Think about some of the people you know. Which ones seem to attract good luck? Which of them seem to always have bad luck? Then spend a minute thinking about what they are like. What are they like when you are around them? Are they optimists, or are they pessimists?

> *"GRACE"*
>
> *GR—GREAT*
> *A—ATTITUDES*
> *C—CHANGE*
> *E—EVERYTHING*
>
> Robert Charles Payne

When I was teaching, I once had a student come into my room with a dejected look. I asked him what was wrong, and he told me that he thought he had just flunked his math test. I told him to think more positively. He then looked at me and said, "Coach Payne, I am positive that I flunked my math test."

I once gave a seminar on television that had to do with having a more positive outlook on life. Several days later, I received a letter from a very angry man. He was infuriated with me for portraying such a positive outlook on life. He wanted to know what day I was going to walk on water so that he could bring his grandchildren to watch.

I told him that he should bring them as soon as the pond freezes over.

Oh, I will be the first to admit that having a positive outlook on life it not a fool-proof formula for enjoying the good fruits of life, but it surely helps. Remember that we all have a choice concerning the way we think.

Overloaded or Over Aged?

Well, it finally happened. Donna and I had a good laugh on me. Donna usually has provided many of the funnies over the years, but today her husband shared with her an incident that brought tears to her eyes. Not tears of sadness, you understand, but a pure, gut-wrenching belly laugh.

My brother, Joe Beck, had come by the house to see if I wanted to ride with him to look at a camp on Lake Darbonne. It was a nice afternoon drive. After looking at the camp, we walked out on the dock, which reminded me of the docks on Lake Bruin. The experience brought back so many memories, from age six all the way to adulthood.

Joe Beck and I were on our way back from the lake when we stopped to get some refreshments. I also purchased two papers, the *Banner* and the *Gazette*. I knew of the *Gazette*, but not the *Banner*, which I found to be the Bernice paper. Now sit down. You will need to.

Since I had never heard of The Banner, I was interested in reading it. I have always enjoyed reading these small town newspapers, and so I was strongly focused on the *Banner*. You know sometimes we subconsciously just walk while our mind is on something else.

When I came out of the store, I turned to my left and walked over to get in the truck. After I had gotten in the truck, I placed the papers on my lap and looked over toward Joe Beck. But there was something terribly wrong. The driver was not Joe Beck but another man with a really shocked look on his face. He never said a word to me. He just kept this startled expression on his face. I looked at him, told him very casually that I was in the wrong truck, and quickly exited. When I headed toward Joe Beck's truck, which was in the opposite direction and almost six vehicles over from the truck that I had visited very briefly, I could see Joe Beck was in stitches.

Donna really enjoyed her chance for a good laugh on her husband. It was not a big deal. I had just gotten into the wrong truck. Did I say I was subconscious or unconscious? There were absolutely no similarities:

1. **Different color.** JB's truck is white. The other was grey.

2. **Different style.** JB's 4X4 extended cab was a Chevrolet. The other was a two-wheel drive Dodge.

3. **Different position.** JB's truck was to the right from the store. The other truck was to the left.

4. **Different year.** JB's was a newer style. The other was an older model.

5. **Different man in the driver's seat.** JB is blonde and wears contacts. The other driver was brunette, had a mustache, and wore glasses.

We have not had a better laugh since the time I turned too quickly one day when I was in a very big hurry to go to the bathroom, only to find out a few minutes later that I had been in the ladies rest room. Well, you decide. Am I overloaded? Or am I over aged? Can I expect some more of these unforeseen events?

Nonetheless, when all is said and done, "Laughter is the best medicine," even if you are the star of the story.

The Magic Ingredients

The most influential book that I have read in my lifetime, with the exception of the Holy Bible, is Napoleon Hill's *Think and Grow Rich*. I have read it nine times, and now I am reading it for the tenth time. I am sixty-two years old. Why would I still be reading *Think and Grow Rich?* The reason is that when I read it, new ideas are always generated—ideas that I use in my columns, in my books, and for my speaking engagements. They are ideas that I hope will enrich the lives of others and keep my own life rich with expectancy.

Although there are some goals and dreams that I will not accomplish, there are still new dreams that are within my grasp if I only

> *"Whatever the mind of man can conceive and believe, it can achieve."*

continue to embrace the magic ingredients leading to the fulfillment of these dreams. Also, giving birth to new dreams adds a lot of excitement and encouragement as I face my senior years.

As the Bible says, "stir the gift." I love to stir the gift each day. It is what I have always called "getting my molecules lined up." When all the molecules are lined up, the word impossible is no longer a part of my vocabulary. And as the book *Think and Grow Rich* states, "Whatever the mind of man can conceive and believe, it can achieve."

There are two magic ingredients that anyone can have. These ingredients are belief and desire. And we all should remember that belief and desire are free—to everyone! You don't have to have money. You don't have to have influence. You don't have to live in the right neighborhood. All that is needed is for you to believe with a burning desire to achieve.

Blair Hill understood. Andrew Grove understood. Jean Dominique Bauby understood. They all understood what the magic ingredients were.

Blair Hill, the son of Napoleon Hill, had no ears when he was born. He went through school not being able to hear his teachers, but his mother and father believed that one day their son would hear. Not only did Blair eventually hear, but he also became very successful selling the product that made his hearing possible.

When Andrew Grove immigrated to America in 1957 and started school, he could not read the headlines of the newspapers or even speak a word of English. However, because he believed and had a burning desire to achieve, he became the valedictorian of his class in three years. Andrew Grove went on to become the CEO of the Intel Corporation. The company's assets grew into billions of dollars and employed thousands.

Jean-Dominique Bauby, a French journalist, suffered a massive stroke that put him in a coma. Three days later, he awoke from the coma to find that the only unaffected muscles were those of his left eye. Nevertheless, he learned to communicate by blinking when someone pointed to a letter of the alphabet. Through dictation by blinking with his left eye, he was able to author a book of 137 pages. Bauby understood the forces of belief and desire.

Whenever we catch ourselves bemoaning the tough situations in our lives, remember that the two ingredients that lead toward the fulfillment of your dreams are free. You could be young and chasing those early dreams, or you could be over sixty like me and birthing new dreams. Age does not matter. The formula for achievement is the same for all of us.

Root System Key to Every Strong Family

We were all sitting on the front porch of my Granddaddy and Grandmother Payne's house. The front porch was the favorite gathering place after we had finished supper, for the night was not complete without some good conversation out on the porch. On this particular night, we had been talking about the Mississippi River.

The Payne family had migrated from Philadelphia, Mississippi, to Crowville, Louisiana, in the early 1900s. During the conversation about the Mississippi River, Grandmother spoke up and said that she had never seen the Mississippi River. Everyone was mystified by her statement, because she and Granddaddy had crossed over the river many times whenever they traveled from Crowville to Philadelphia and back on family visits.

Granddaddy said, "Momma, what do you mean that you have never seen the Mississippi River? You have been with me many times when we crossed the Mississippi."

"Yeah, Poppa. But you were driving, and I never looked at the river because I was afraid you would look too."

How many of you are old enough to remember that old bridge at Vicksburg? It was a scary time when you were crossing that narrow bridge with lanes that were only wide enough for old Model T Fords. The highway was so small that if you did take your eyes off the road for just a second, you did have a very good chance of running into another car or, as Grandmother thought, into the river. But there was nothing scarier than crossing that bridge at the same time a train was crossing. The railroad tracks were right there beside you. It reminded me of the times when we rode

Shetland ponies at my Granddaddy Beck's cattle farm during a cattle roundup. When I rode by those cows, I was looking up at their bellies. That was about the same feeling that I got when our car was next to a train crossing the Mississippi River Bridge. I was looking up at the bellies of all the box cars. They looked big and close, too close, especially to a little boy.

As I stated earlier, the bridge at Vicksburg was built for the old T-models. The newer and bigger automobiles of the fifties caused a tight squeeze. I was like my grandmother: I did not enjoy crossing that bridge either.

There are many stories we can share that we heard while visiting our grandmother and granddaddy. Grandparents' houses have always appealed to the grandkids. I am sure that if you ask people where one of their favorite places was during their childhood, they would say grandmother and granddaddy's. Grandkids never ran out of things to do in the country.

Usually when we went to Crowville, all my daddy's brothers and sisters and their families would come over. We would always have a huge dinner with some of the best cooking this country has ever known. The conversations during the meals were as good as all the food.

After lunch, everybody grabbed a chair and moved the visiting out under the big oak tree. I remember those big roots that reached out and gave that big old tree a solid foundation to help it withstand storms. The roots of that big tree are much like the roots that reach out from our own family tree. That root system is the key to the strength of the foundation of every family.

I will always cherish that big oak tree and what it represents, but I still wonder if Grandmother ever saw the Mississippi River.

The Compound Interest on Thinking

When there has been a traumatic incident in your life, coming as a result of someone else's transgression and lacking forgiveness as a part of the formula for healing, then the compounding of this tragic experience begins. It is no different from the compounding of interest on money. The longer you carry the incident around with you, the greater the result of its consequences. When you make the event a part of your everyday conversation, the compounding of this experience continues to grow. The compounding formula works as well in our thought processes as it does in economics.

Have you ever come to the point where an experience has become a part of every family discussion? Has it ever become a regular part of breakfast, lunch, and supper, and you actually begin to eat your words as they become a part of your mental consumption? The result is very damaging, both mentally and physically. As you have heard people say, "It has begun to take its toll." It has become the dominant force in your life, creating an almost inescapable, downward trend. Gloom and doom. Why do bad things always happen to me? I will never let him get away with it. I was wronged. Poor me. Then the black devil "depression" takes control of your life. The negative cycle has become so strong that it has become like a tornado destroying everything in the path of your life.

What is so bad about this negative cycle is that the forces of negativity begin to draw other forces of negativity, and again the compound effect takes place. The destruction caused by these emotional storms can place a person in the pits of despair. What began as an innocent reaction toward the person or persons who wronged you has not resulted in your decision to consciously not forgive someone. Whether we are aware of it or not, the resulting bitterness has led to a troubling, descending trend, creating an emotional trap that can wreak havoc in our lives.

Don't ever think that forgiveness is only for the other person. The act of forgiving is for you as well. The moment that you forgive someone, you have been released from your emotional prison. Now this decision is not magic that will cause all the effects to go away, but once you decide to forgive, then you can slowly begin with the restoration from all the storms.

You have heard people say to "forgive and forget." All this does is make one feel guilty. Trying to forget the trauma is another trauma in itself, but learning to forgive is the elixir of life.

> *"Going against the crowd is a universal principle that produces rewards in all areas of our lives, not just the invisible."*—*"To those who have, more shall be given."*
>
> Ken Roberts

We all battle with the issue of forgiveness. I am great at forgiving someone when life is going great, but should another incident come up, I will take it back. There have been several incidents in my life that I have had to forgive, forgive, forgive, and forgive until I got it right. You will know when you are sincere about forgiving someone because, at that moment, you will feel a powerful emotional release from all the heavy burdens that you have carried for so long.

Now you can close your negative accounts and open new accounts where you can deposit your positive thoughts on a daily basis. These daily deposits begin to accumulate new assets that begin to eliminate old liabilities. As the compounding increases, your interest in life increases. You can "bank on it."

Smiles Add Miles to Life

Our first story is about two farmers. One farmer was the eternal optimist, and the other farmer was the eternal pessimist. When it rained, the optimist would always praise the cool rain and how it watered beautifully all God's creations. The pessimist would grumble that the water would probably drown everything around. When the sun shone, the optimist would comment on the beauty of the magnificent sun rays, while the pessimist complained that the sun would probably dry everything up.

One day, the optimist went out and bought a Labrador Retriever. This was no ordinary dog: the retriever could walk on water. Instead of swimming after the ducks, the unusual dog would walk across the top of the water to get them and bring them back. The optimist thought that he would cheer up his pessimistic friend and invited him for a duck hunt. The optimist could not wait to show his friend what this dog could do. So early the next morning, the two went out hunting. When they had shot down their first ducks, the optimist turned to the pessimist and said, "Watch this. Go, boy." And the dog stepped out on the water, began walking across it, picked up the ducks, and walked back across the water to the two men. The optimist turned to the pessimist and asked, "What do you think of that?" The pessimist looked at the optimist and said with his usual pessimism, "Can't swim, can he?"

The next story shows that the optimist is always looking for the solutions and not the problems. There was a Chinese grocery store owner. A large chain had been buying up all the grocery stores and property around him. Everyone was selling to the large chain except for him. When he was approached with another offer, the Chinese grocer said no. The large chain owners then made another offer and told him that it would be their last one; if he turned it down, they would build around him. He turned them down again, and they soon had him surrounded.

When they were finally set for the big day, he was right in the middle of it. They had banners flying everywhere: "Grand Opening." The Chinese grocer put up his own banner the day of his competitor's grand opening. His banner was right over his little store, which was in the middle of all their new buildings and their grand opening. The Chinese grocer walked out of his store and pulled the cord so that all could see his banner: "Main Entrance!"

Laughter certainly makes every day brighter. I hope the next few lines will also keep your tickle box turned over:

A couple had gone to the store to buy some furniture. A salesman approached them to try to make a sale. He said to them, "You don't pay anything down, and you don't pay anything for a year." The wife jumped back, "Who told you about us?"

Did you hear about the man who was run over by a steam roller? He is in room 105, 106, 107, and 108 . . .

An employee who was hospitalized received a card from his fellow workers who had wished him a speedy recovery by a 77 to 75 vote. And that was on the second ballot.

"Forgive us for our trash baskets as we forgive those who put trash in our baskets."—Quote from a four-year-old.

When does a woman enjoy a man's company? When he owns it.

There have been scientific studies proving that laughter and smiles do add miles to your life. So smile, smile, smile.

Thank You, Daddy

He was a country boy from Crowville. His parents had taught him a way of life that was guided by honesty, humility, and a caring heart for his fellow man. He was especially partial to those who were considered underdogs—the underprivileged. He came from a family of nine children. Two of his sisters died at a young age. One drowned in the Beough River, and the other died of scarlet fever.

God had blessed him with a lot of athletic talent. In fact, he was so fast that he had acquired the nickname "Speedy" in Crowville. He was chosen as an All-Stater in high school, but all the colleges said he was too small. However, he did not let that deter him from trying to play on the collegiate level. He caught a bus to Nachitoches to try to play for the Northwestern State Demons. When they told him that he was too small for college ball, he caught the next ride and headed for Pineville to try out for Louisiana College.

Yes, he was too small, but that did not keep him from earning All-American honors and being considered, at only 163 pounds, one of the best running backs in the nation. Unfortunately, he came along at the wrong time for the pros. Running backs that were only five-feet-nine-inches tall were not given a chance to play. Thank goodness Marshall Faulk, Charlie Tolar, Emmitt Smith, Barry Sanders, and Tony Dorsett did not come along in those days when any running back under six feet tall was considered too short for the NFL. So Devone Payne did the next best thing: he coached.

In the 1940s, he arrived in Tallulah and immediately became one of the rising stars in the coaching profession. He coached with the same ability and enthusiasm with which he had performed as a player. I could fill this essay with all the stats for his teams, but there are many coaches with great records. Nonetheless, I am proud of how he cared for his players. I have wonderful memories of going to all the ball games and watching Coach Payne pacing back and forth on the sidelines in his patented brown suit.

Daddy died on March 21, 1958, while he was the head coach at Northeast. But you see, what is remarkable is that in his short tenure before his death, he had taken Northeast to another level with his staff of three. The pain of losing my father was quite difficult. But our mother, widowed at thirty-seven years of age with four boys (two teenagers and two toddlers), kept his memory alive. We lived everyday through memories of his relationships with his players, his friends, his church, his extended family, and most of all, his wife.

We had a very large extended family. There were approximately a thousand of us. Our big family came from Crowville, Tallulah, Pineville, and Monroe.

What made my daddy such a successful individual was his desire to have such a large family. There has not been a day that has gone by since his death that I have not had a chance to be with one of our family members.

I was able to see a lot more of my family on April 21, 2007. They came over for dinner as we inducted Coach Devone Payne into the ULM Hall of Fame.

Thank you, Daddy, for you and Momma deciding to have such a big family.

Take Time to Examine the Little Things

When I was in the coaching profession, I always taught my players that it was the little things that make a great difference. What is the difference between being barely alive and being barely dead? There is a great difference. Ladies, what is the difference between being barely pregnant and not being pregnant? Quite a lot. How much difference is there between barely catching a plane and barely missing a plane? Similarly, how much difference is there between barely landing on the runway and barely missing the runway? You see, there is a great big difference.

I always observe how well people take care of the little things. Whenever I was offered a coaching position, I always would arrive early before talking to the principal. I would go to a gas station (this was when an attendant pumped gas for you), put in a few dollars worth (this was also when you could get several gallons for a dollar), and talk to the man who was pumping gas into my car. I would ask him questions about the high school, the football team, the principal, and the community. I learned much through these informal interviews while getting gasoline put into my tank. In one town, I asked the man why the football coach had been fired. He answered, "Wrong religion." I quickly asked him, "What religion was he?" I was safe: the former coach was from another denomination.

After pumping gas, I had one more place to go before I met with the principal. I would visit the restrooms at the high school. I had discovered this test years ago, maybe from my own father. Although I am not sure where I picked this up, it was a true litmus test of how good a job the principal was doing and what kind of leader he was. I would always check the bathrooms before I met with anybody. If they were spotless, I knew there was a person running the show who understood that the little things make a great big difference. If the bathrooms were dirty, I could return to my car before being seen and go to the nearest phone to tell the principal that I was not able to accept the job. Yes, it was also the days before the cell phone.

In the beginning of the McDonald's franchises, their successes depended on this same philosophy concerning restrooms. When McDonald's first began, there were no high-tech ways of running the numbers. You had to have your own litmus test. McDonald's made it a high priority to have clean restrooms. In the early days of McDonald's, they catered to traveling families, and there was one thing people wanted to have for their families when they stopped—very clean restrooms. The little things make a great big difference, for McDonald's became a giant hamburger chain.

Another "high"-tech method they used before building a new McDonald's was to go up in an airplane and count the church steeples. Wherever the steeples were clustered is where the new McDonald's would be built in that area. It is the little things that count.

This week, treat everyone you meet as if he is the most important person in the world. You will see. It is the little things that make a big difference.

Standing on the Top Looking Down

I celebrated my sixty-fifth birthday on March 29. I don't have nearly as much time in front of me as I have already put behind me.

I heard a man say one time that he was not "over the hill" but "on top, looking down." I figure that it is better to be "on top, looking down" than to be "on the bottom, looking up." Most of us who have reached the fourth quarter of our game of life are aware that we do spend time retracing some of the journey as the journey nears the end.

I think back to the most traumatic moment of my young life. It was when I was called into the office of my principal, Dr. Sidney Seegers, and he and my coach, Van Leigh, were there waiting for me. Since I had never been called out of my classroom and told to report to the office, I was not sure if I was in trouble about something or what exactly was going on. I can still remember how hard it was for those two men to put on a face that would not cause me concern. I don't know if they had ever been called upon to make such an announcement to a student, but I am sure that it is not something to which anyone would look forward. They had to tell me that my father had just died.

I relate to this story because, as I look back on the years of my life, I think of the men and women who were there for me during difficult times. There were football coaches and teachers who made a difference. I shudder to think what

> *"The level of our emotional pain is in direct proportion to how much we are covering up."*
>
> *Dancing in the Dawn*

would have happened if my coaches had not served as surrogate fathers through my junior high, high school, and college days. These men went beyond the call of duty to give of their time and make sure that the adjustments in the face of trauma were made easier.

Some years ago, Dr. Seegers, the superintendent of the Monroe City school system, introduced me as the speaker at a teachers' meeting. Even though it had been more than thirty years from the day that he had had to tell a thirteen-year-old boy that his father had just died, he still had to fight back the tears of memories as he introduced me as the guest speaker. My heart embraced Dr. Seegers because I too remembered that day as if it were only yesterday. After Lee Junior High, Dr. Seegers and I had gone to Neville High School together. He had been named as the new principal, and I was a brand new freshman. Coaches Bill Ruple, Charlie Brown, and "Chick" Childress, guiding me through my high school years, were added to my list of surrogate fathers. Coach Jim Coates, who had been a very close friend of my daddy's, became my coach at Northeast. My only offer to play college ball came from Northeast. No one else thought I was big enough to play at this level. Not only did Coach Coates think that I was big enough to play, but he also thought that I was good enough to start as a freshman—and I did.

Red Sims was the only one who stepped in for my younger brother, Joe Beck. Red took him to Jefferson Junior High in the seventh grade. Did Red have to take Joe Beck to school? We lived out by the college. Red lived out in the west Ouachita area. I know that you must be thinking Red must have done this for athletic purposes, but you can rest assured that Red did not take Joe Beck because he was a big hulk who could help the football team. Joe Beck might have weighed eighty pounds soaking wet. Red took Joe Beck to school with him because he wanted to help a young boy who had lost his father.

I share these stories to illustrate the Biblical injunction that we are to take care of the widows and the fatherless. These men proved that true Christianity reaches far beyond Sunday mornings. They did their part far beyond the reach of the church. My mother, brothers, and I were one family who were fortunate enough to have been the recipients of applied Christianity.

As the television advertisement says, "How much was it worth? Priceless."

Never Throw in the
Towel on Your Dreams

Do you think that there is ever a time in life when we should "throw in the towel" and give up on our dreams? When we were children, we all had big dreams. There was no doubt that we could become what we desired to be, but as life's experiences began to take their toll, we pulled in our dream wings. As we age, we don't fly as far and as high as we once did. We think that life has passed us by. Maybe our marriage didn't work out. Maybe we lost our job. Maybe we got passed over by others on the way to the top of the ladder. Maybe our financial goals never materialized. Our disappointments over broken dreams have only added weight to our already overloaded life. Added to all the disillusionment, the biggest tragedy of all is when we think that we have gotten too old and that life has passed us by.

I love to read my Bible, not because I am such a righteous man, but because I need all the wisdom and guidance I can find. One particular Bible story that offers great wisdom and guidance is about a man whose life appeared to be over when he was forty. He had been a very high-profile public official, recognized throughout the nation, and the son of the head of the government.

As a young boy, and later as a young man, he had lived a privileged life. He had had the best of everything, and one day he would be the leader of the nation. But as life has a tendency to do to us sometimes, it threw him a curveball, and he missed it. He killed a man that he thought was abusing a slave; but

> *"One today is worth two tomorrows."*
> Ben Franklin

instead of people coming to his defense for rescuing the slave, he had to leave the country to escape punishment.

God "benched" him at forty. He spent the next forty years in exile, where he became a farmer with his father-in-law and raised his family. His ways and styles of living changed. His importance waned, and he settled into complete anonymity, growing comfortable with his new life and environment.

Then something happened. God called him to "go back into the game" at eighty years of age. However, He did not put him in just any position. God put him in as the quarterback—the leader. God wanted him to lead the team to the greatest come-from-behind victory in history. For forty years he had learned to live off the land. Now he would teach a nation how to live off the land. No one had ever been able to lead his team to victory from such a seemingly insurmountable deficit so late in the game.

Yes, Moses had been benched at forty, not because God was finished with him, but only because God wanted to train him for forty more years. Sometimes when life has taken a peculiar turn, it is not because God is finished with us. Our plans and God's plans are so different. If you think that your life is over, if you think that God has forgotten you, if you think that you are too old, and if you think it is too late for you to be what God has put you here to be, remember the story of Moses. Moses thought that his life was over at forty, when in reality, the first seventy-nine years were only preparation for one of the greatest roles of leadership in the history of mankind.

No one should ever feel that life is over. No matter what you are facing, or what your age may be, God only begins to use us when we are seasoned enough to start listening and mature enough to heed the instructions.

Learning Lessons
from the Natural World

One day last week as I was walking around our circle in Darbonne Hills in West Monroe, Louisiana (we don't have blocks; we have circles), I noticed all the beauty created by the greatest artist there has ever been—God. Who else could have mixed such beautiful colors? Who else could have created all of the pastel coloring? Who else could have made a variety of shades instead of only one kind of red, blue, green, pink, orange, white, yellow, or violet? God made many colors, each with several different tints. There is no dullness in God's paintings.

Each morning as I begin my walk, I first notice the light of the sun, the reflections, the shadows, and the clouds. There is nothing as silent as a cloud moving quietly through the sky, changing its shapes before moving out of sight. Then the sounds of happiness are everywhere. All the birds are singing, chirping in a language of their own. "Pretty bird. Pretty bird," is the language of the cardinal. The mockingbird's voice seems to be in several languages. There are "cheerp, cheerps, cheep, cheeps" and the various tones of whistling. There is one universal message coming from all of these winged creatures: they all wake up happy. They love to meet the morning. They fly from one limb to another and one tree to another as if they were already visiting their neighborhood friends, but it does seem that all neighborhoods have got that one unhappy grouch. For birds, it is that old crow with his irritating sound of discontent: "Awkkk! Awkkk!" Does that old sound remind you of anyone?

Then, by the shrill whistle of the hawk out looking for its prey, I am reminded each morning of the danger that lurks in each of our lives. Even with all the beauty that God has created, there is that threatening part of His creation, that balance of good and evil. That is the part of creation we don't fully understand. Why do bad things happen to good people? We can spend our lives trying to explain this phenomenon of balance, but only when we enter into the Heavenly Kingdom will we understand creation, birth, death, happiness, unhappiness, pain, joy, and all the antagonistic distractions called opposites or life's opposing forces.

My walk begins about the time the squirrels have come out to play, chasing each other around the trees or sprinting from one tree to the next. Sometimes I will hear one bark from a perch on a limb as if she wants to get my attention. Then she begins shaking her tail like a cheerleader with pom-poms to see if I will stop and watch her morning pep rally.

What I have noticed most about God's creatures is that they are so happy to begin their day. Most of God's creatures seem to feel this way. Isn't it ironic that the creature that is supposed to be most like God is the unhappiest of all his creations?

Momma Knows What Is Good for You

The following speeches are excerpts from the eulogies given by the four sons of Dr. DeLores Beck Payne on the day of her funeral, January 10, 1992.

"Today I consider myself to be the luckiest person on earth. For almost fifty years, I have been the boy to have never failed at anything that I tried to do. I always made straight A's and pretty much led a near perfect life because that was what my Momma told me, so it has to be true. But now that I think about that, there is a slight flaw in my thinking, because it was Momma who walked the walk and talked the talk. She was God's example of a kinder, gentler person. She was the 'thousand points of light' for four boys, their families, and all others who knew her. If you paid attention, you could see that she was using a higher curve for her grades than she used for others. Her family gave her an A. Her friends gave her an A. I am sure God gave her an A; and when it is all said and done, what else counts? She was the most giving and forgiving person I have ever known, and I hope that some day I can be graded on her curve and can be the kind of winner that she was."— Devone, the oldest.

"I hope that I can finish with what I think everyone should know about my mother. She was not only my mother; she also was my father, too. I don't think that I could ask for better ones either. She was my teacher, my coach, my motivator, and my best friend. I don't think I remember my father, because I was only two when he passed away; but boy, do I remember him in the memories that Momma shared. Momma never let him die in our lives. She always put everyone else first. She would do without to give me something I wanted or needed. I wish everyone could have a mother like the one that I had for thirty-six years. I am proud to be her son."—Andy, the youngest son.

"Mother wore many hats: wife, mother, grandmother, great-grandmother, professor, teacher, widow, friend, aunt, daughter, and sister. My mother was a giver, but today is her day, and we are here to give to her what she has given to so many others."—Joe Beck, next to the youngest son.

"Our mother wore many hats. She was a silent motivator. She was a great seed planter. She was a courageous woman. She never complained. She was a devout Christian woman. An achiever. A totally unselfish person."—Robert Charles, next to the oldest.

I am sure that many of you feel the same about your mother. Sunday is Mother's Day. It is her day. If your Mother is still alive, send her some flowers or take her out to eat. If your mother lives too far away to visit, make sure that you give her a phone call. And most of all, say, "Mom, I love you."

I Was Addressed as
"Dr. Robert Charles Payne"

On March 22, 1989, I obtained proof that I had my doctorate degree from the State of Louisiana from the Board of Elementary and Secondary Education. At least the envelope was addressed to Dr. Robert Charles Payne. I told my mother, who worked very hard to earn her doctorate, that she had put in too much time. All that I had done was apply for the job of state superintendent, and immediately I was addressed as Dr. Robert Charles Payne. So with my Ph.D. in hand, I do feel qualified to make some statements concerning the learning process. Seriously though, I do want to share some ideas about the potential found in every one of us.

Having been a classroom teacher for almost fourteen years, having been the student of unbelievably gifted mentors, and having spent almost forty-five years of serious research on education, motivation, learning, and people skills, I now focus upon trying to impact the fields of learning and motivation. When I retired and reached sixty years of age, my passion for life-long dreams was reignited. Now I have the time to pursue this mission that I have carried in my heart for as long as I can remember.

One belief that I had as a teacher was that one cannot force a child to learn or reach him extrinsically. One must motivate the child until he causes a small spark that lights the fires of desire. When that intrinsic part of the child is awakened, he will have a desire to learn—a desire so strong that his appetite for knowledge will be insatiable.

His drive now comes from within, not without. The key to stirring the gifts within is for the teacher to learn what motivates a child. It is this latent, hidden mystery that lies asleep inside every child, waiting to be awakened. The legendary coach of UCLA, John Wooden, stated that you haven't taught until they have learned.

I found over the years that students don't make bad grades because they are dumb. Students make bad grades because they hurt. Grades are not representative of degrees of intelligence, but only representative of to what degree the child understands the subject matter as presented by the teacher. If we give a child the right keys at the right time, he can unlock his own potential.

And just what is potential? The entire works of William Shakespeare translated into 200 languages can be sent from New York to Omaha, Nebraska, without skipping a verse in 0.043 seconds. This is the potential that can be found in the speed of light. How does this compare to the potential found in a student? Maybe we should ask Helen Keller, Ludwig van Beethoven, William Lear, Albert Einstein, Bill Gates, Winston Churchill, Oprah Winfrey, Jim Halsell, George Washington Carver, Brett Favre, Ray Charles, Billy Graham, Abraham Lincoln, Jonas Salk, Thomas Edison, Benjamin Franklin, Walt Disney, or those who signed the Declaration of Independence. These men and women represent the potential in every student that sits in the classroom. And what do all these people have in common? They are ordinary people who had the sleeping giant awakened within them, and they unleashed this unlimited potential to become extraordinary people. More simply stated, they were common people who learned to do uncommon things.

There is unlimited potential in every student sitting in the classroom. I tip my hat and give the highest admiration and respect to the teacher who knows how to tap that source of unlimited potential and reveal the secret of the giant within. I offer the challenge to all: stir the gift.

Never Giving Up
Only Makes You Stronger

Have you ever been told that you could not do something? For some people, that command only strengthens their resolve to prove otherwise. I heard a story some years ago about a young boy that was told he was too little to play football. The coach told him to go home because they did not have a uniform small enough to fit him. He went home and told his mother. Since his mother did not believe in dream killers, she made him a uniform and then took him back to the coach, who immediately let him join the team. This little boy grew to become a great athlete. He started for the University of Oklahoma as an offensive lineman. Oklahoma won several national championships with this little boy, who had grown to 6'4" and weighed 265 pounds. (This was before the days of weight programs. No telling what he would weigh in today's environment.) When he graduated from OU, he went to play for the Green Bay Packers. This little boy who grew into a gentle giant, except for when he was on the football field, is Leon Manley, former football coach at NLU. Coach Manley retired when he was on the staff with Darrel Royal at the University of Texas. Coach Manley was not only a great football player, but he was also one of the finest role models in the coaching profession.

Another story concerning resolve is about a young man who was taken out of school at thirteen years of age because he was too slow to learn. The experts told him he could only do minimal work, and he went to work for his brother, a medical doctor who owned a sanitarium. He considered himself his brother's flunky. Although he developed a cereal for the sanitarium, his doctor brother rejected the idea for a commercial venture. Not allowing this rejection to discourage him, he stepped out of his brother's shadow and went out on his own at the age of forty-six. His name is Will Kellogg. From his one idea was born Kellogg's Corn Flakes.

What do you do with a child that did not talk until he was five and did not learn to read until he was seven? Parents, don't get worried if your child lags behind. He may just be taking the same path as Albert Einstein.

Rose Blukin, an immigrant, came to the United States in 1917 totally penniless. Later, her husband died when she was forty-three. How does a forty-three-year-old widow face such tragedy? She borrowed five hundred dollars and began the Nebraska Furniture Company, which became one of America's largest furniture companies.

Another slow learner was Thomas Edison. Edison holds thousands of trademarks on inventions.

If anyone should have quit, it should have been James Robinson. Although he was conceived during a rape, he became one of American's great evangelists. Now Jim and his wife, Betty, have their own international television ministry.

All the aforementioned people had a reason to quit, but they all had the tenacity and drive to overcome whatever was placed in their way. The passion and the will to succeed were characteristics of each of them.

Memories of My Yesterday

My morning walks always stir my memory pool. The beauty of the early mornings gives birth to the best of thoughts, which return to the days at my grandparents' home. My daddy was a country boy raised on a little farm a few miles from Crowville, Louisiana, until he left for college in the 1930s. Later, this little farm became the center for all the families of the brothers and sisters to gather for many years to come. The peace that was a by-product of the simplicity of the times brought a happiness that created excitement when it was time to go to Grandmother and Granddaddy Payne's.

There were no Toy's R Us stores or Wal-Marts. If you wanted a toy, you created it from your imagination. I loved to play "cars" under the house. Those country homes were raised off of the ground several feet. This made for an ideal playground. We could make roads in the dirt for our cars. Our toy cars were anything from bricks, rocks, or bottles. I always sought out the milk of magnesia bottle. These bottles were dark blue and made the coolest looking cars. Of course, you always got out of the way of those brick trucks. They could break any bottle cars.

If we got bored around the house, we could go into the woods in the front of the house to play on the "flying Jennie." For those of you who are not from the country or not over sixty years of age, a "flying Jennie" was a tree that had been cut down, its stump sharpened with a point so that the trunk of the tree, which had a hole hollowed out in its middle, could be positioned to fit over the sharp stump. Then we could sit on each end of the trunk and go around and around like a merry-go-round. Who needs an expensive swing set?

Another game was "washers." You dug two small holes in the ground several feet from each other. Using several washers from farm machinery, you tried to see how many washers that you could get into the hole at the other end. When night rolled around, you could then start the night games—playing kick the can, hide and seek, or dirt wars in the cotton fields, or throwing dirt clods at the bats.

And, of course, there were the favorite pastimes. We could go squirrel or coon hunting with Queenie, Uncle Rufus's blood-hound. If we wanted to hunt rabbits, we would use my cousin Fabian's dog Flip Flop. Or we would hunt ducks on Uncle Talmadge's pond. Since I was never a cold weather fisherman, we fished in Uncle Talmadge's or Uncle Jay's ponds during the summertime. There was plenty for us to do.

Who could forget those big dinners with fried chicken, rabbit, and squirrel? Furthermore, there was always a multitude of side dishes and desserts, such as butter beans, black-eyed peas, okra, corn on the cob, beets, squash, egg plant, cucumbers, tomatoes, fruit salad, cake, pies, watermelon, homemade ice cream, fried pies, and iced tea—and this was only one meal. No wonder I miss those good times in the country a few miles from Crowville, Louisiana. The house is gone, but the memories remain of the times when our families came together in the curve of the gravel road at the country residence of our daddy's mom and dad.

Yes, it is the simple things that keep us anchored during times that move so rapidly our identities almost become a blur. These anchors have been carved from the family tree of strong, hard-working country folk who kept their family as number one in life's pursuits; because of their God-centered way of living, the anchor still holds.

Have You Ever Wondered
If God Plays Football?

Have you ever wondered if God plays football? He could very well be involved, but I don't think that He ever takes sides. But sometimes I wonder. One of the most inspiring stories that I have ever heard was told to me by the late Bill Ruple. Neville was in the play-offs with DeQuincy High School. Back in those days, there was not enough money to carry all the players to the out-of-town games. Thursdays were usually set aside for a short pre-game practice. After practice was finished on Thursday and all the players had packed their bags and gone home, Ruple was checking to make sure that all the equipment was ready for the trip when he saw one player still hanging around. Ruple noticed that the young man was red-eyed from crying. When Ruple asked him what was bothering him, the player told Coach Ruple that he wanted so badly to get to dress out and go to the game, but he was not on the travel list. All of you who were acquainted with Coach Ruple know that his heart melted when he saw a teary-eyed kid. When Ruple saw how much the kid wanted to go, he told him, "Oh, you can go. You can have my seat. I'll stand in the stairwell. Go get yourself packed."

Neville and DeQuincy had battled all night that Friday night. DeQuincy had a 12 to 0 lead with time running out. Neville scored late in the game to make it 12 to 7. By the time Neville was set to kick-off, one of Neville's players had been hurt on the play before, and there were only ten men on the field. When Ruple noticed that they were one man short, he grabbed the player nearest to him and sent him into the game. Now what happened next might make you wonder if God does play at times. Neville kicked-off, and the player whom Ruple had inserted at the last minute went down, made the tackle, and caused a fumble that Neville recovered. Neville took the ball and marched it down for a score that won the game. Who was the player that Ruple had inserted at the last minute? It was the same young man for whom Ruple had made a place the day before. What do you think? Does God play football?

On another occasion, my wife and I were attending a West Monroe play-off game. At that time in West Monroe's history, play-offs were rare. West Monroe was playing Carencro, who had a great player by the name of Kevin Faulk. It was late in the game, and West Monroe had less than a touchdown lead. Faulk took the ball and started on a sweep. He had made the corner and had daylight all the way to the goal, but as he broke into the open, he left the ball behind. Faulk had to run the ball quite often, and he did not respond quickly to the fumble. I am not sure he even knew that he had dropped the ball. West Monroe recovered the ball to preserve the victory in the quarter finals.

Why do I think that this particular play was monumental for West Monroe? I remember leaning over to my wife and saying, "Donna, they are going to win it all." And win it all they did, for West Monroe won its first state championship. I believe this play in this one moment gave birth to one of the most outstanding programs in America.

Getting a Kick Out of Life Way Back When

Since I have had several days lately when my mind has been on a negative trend, I have had to continue to reach into the vaults of my memories to allow the light to shine more brightly. When I was at Neville High School, I kicked field goals. Let me rephrase that. I kicked at field goals. And how did I become the field goal kicker?

One afternoon after our pre-game on Thursday, I stayed after practice by myself to practice kicking extra points. I placed the ball on a kicking tee and kicked quite a few extra points. I decided to try kicking some field goals to see how far I could kick. I think that I finally got back as far as the thirty-five yard line, which is a forty-five yard field goal— not too bad. Little did I know that Coach Ruple had been watching me without my knowledge.

The next night, we were winning the game by a big margin, but Ruple never enjoyed just beating up on another team. We were ahead by four touchdowns, and the second and third teams had played most of the night. When we were on the forty-five yard line with a first and ten, I was standing next to Coach Ruple on the side lines, and he handed me the kicking tee. "Here. Go kick a field goal." I had never attempted a field goal in a game in my life. This would be a fifty-five yarder. Of course I didn't make it. Nor did I make any of the next four attempts, which were all over forty years. I kept the huddle in stitches as I called the plays for each field goal: "Okay, field goal. Return right." Or, "Field goal, open up a hole between the tackle and end so the ball can get through." In other words, I did not kick the ball very far or very high. The lineman had to run down the field in a hurry to keep the other team from returning my field goal attempt for a touchdown. Ruple must have felt assured that I would not add any points to our already four touchdown lead.

I also continued as an outstanding kicker for Northeast Louisiana University when I was a freshman punter. I still hold the record for the "shortest" punt. Yes, the shortest punt—nine yards. I was not the regular punter. We had a young man called "Mile High" Kelley. He could kick it a mile up in the air, but the coaches were not ever sure how far it would go. Our coach had asked me while we were standing on the side line if I thought that I could get the ball out of bounds inside the twenty. What is a freshman going to say? "No, coach, I can't do that"? Of course a freshman is going to assure his coach that he can get it out of bounds. I did kick the ball out of bounds—nine yards down the field. My brother Devone was in the game at the same time, and I'll never forget him turning around after my towering kick of nine yards and saying to me, "You stupid freshman." Do you know how hard it is to try to disappear in the middle of a football field?

Oh, yes. Always remember: records are made to be broken. However, I think that I still hold this record, even after forty-three years. In fact, it could be the longest-standing record in Northeast history.

Stephen King Must
Have Been a Deer Hunter

I was introduced to deer hunting at a very young age. My father was from the school of getting into the woods hours before daylight to allow the scent to weaken. It always seemed that it took hours and hours for daylight to arrive. When Daddy dropped me off at my stand, which was on the ground back then, I would clear out the leaves by a tree and sit down. If there was a stump or a fallen tree, I would be lucky enough to sit above the ground. I always carried a peanut butter sandwich because it would be awhile before anyone would come back to get me. The only problem was that I usually had eaten my sandwich by eight or nine o'clock.

Now you must understand that I had a gun, but it did not lessen my fear of all those creatures I heard before daylight. Back in the 40s and 50s, before bean fields cleared the big woods, there were bears, panthers, wildcats, and other animals that only my imagination could create. I heard things walking out there in the dark that would make a Stephen King movie seem mild. Hearing the scream of a panther would lead me immediately into prayer and a quick rededication of my life.

> "My soul finds a staircase to heaven when I sit in my deer stand."
> Robert Charles Payne

Also back in those days, we did not have the insulated hunting clothing that we have today. I usually had on forty-two pairs of pajamas and fourteen pairs of socks, and I walked like a knight in armor. Have you ever tried to shoot a gun with all of this garb? If you could get the gun up to your shoulder, the next challenge was finding the

79

trigger. It really did not make any difference by this time whether I saw a deer or not; I had spent most of the morning praying for the sun to come up. I needed two things to happen: first, I needed to get warm; second, I needed light to make all those monsters go away.

Believe it or not, I grew up loving to hunt deer, duck, rabbit, squirrel, and dove; and when nothing else was moving, I even enjoyed the chee chee birds. There were two rules that Daddy had made for our hunting. First, don't waste the wildlife. In other words, don't shoot anything that we can't eat. Second, we could not have any dog that could not hunt for supper. I guess the rules have changed about our dogs. Since I have been married, we have had three poodles and one English bulldog. We must have switched from hunting dogs to entertainment dogs, even though our poodles would tree squirrels and our English bulldog would tree people.

When I became an adult, I no longer went into the woods that early. One night, a friend called and asked me to go hunting the next morning. I told him that I could go but that I was not going to go early. He picked me up around eight. When we got to the woods, he dropped me off at my stand and left for his. As I sat down, I noticed a deer slipping through the ravine. I already had my deer before my friend even got to his stand. Ever since I grew up, I have never wanted to sit on my stand any longer than is necessary. This was what I considered an ideal hunt. Hunting has given me many great memories.

It's Okay to Tell Dad You Love Him

On March 20, 1958, we buried our father. That day, I was introduced to the real world. Up until that point, I had usually read about other people facing tragedy—not me. I learned what it was like to walk back into the house after the funeral to realize that Daddy was no longer there.

Life has a way of teaching harsh lessons. I did not know why God didn't take the drunk instead of my father. Over the next forty-nine years, I would learn how good a man he was. He had built a legacy of high standards. It was a challenge for his four boys to learn to live under the same rules, but I would much rather have a name to live up to than a name that would pull me down.

As a father, he was tough, but never did we doubt his love for us. Behind that tough exterior was a soft-hearted and kind man. He was a humble country boy, and he treated everyone with the same respect, whether the person was the mayor or the unemployed. If we wanted to get into trouble fast, we let our father catch us not speaking to someone or not waving to others as we passed—black or white, especially if they were poor. My childhood memories have always served to encourage me when I feel that life has taken a downturn and my journey is not going in the direction that I had expected.

Talking to his former ball players has always brought me a lot of enjoyment. Daddy had an unbelievable rapport with his players even though he was a tough and strict disciplinarian. What took me years to realize was that during the forties and fifties many of his players were headed for the army and sent off to war. I guess boot camp was a breeze after playing four years for Coach Payne. Someone once told me that Daddy was a tough coach, to which I replied, "He was a tough daddy."

The compliments have never stopped since the day that he died. Several years ago, Coach Jim Coates and his wife were being honored on their birthdays. During the party, one of Daddy's former players who had played for him in the fifties said to me, "Robert Charles, your daddy was my best friend." I have heard many compliments given to former coaches, but for one of his players to identify him as his best friend is one of the highest compliments that a coach can receive.

I am sixty-five years old, and I have never quit missing my father. I would love to visit and talk. I would love to take him hunting. I would love to take him for a ride on the Mississippi River levee. I would love to talk to him about coaching. If he had been here, his presence would have stopped me from making the biggest mistake of my life. Daddy knew that if you learn what it is that you love and do it, happiness will follow. Don't ever let Father's Day pass without telling your father that you love him.

True Reality Includes Taste of Failure

When you reach sixty-five years of age, you realize there are some dreams that will not be reached. One of my dreams was to have a class within our educational curriculum that would lead our young students to live successful lives. This could be accomplished by surrounding them with related material such as videos, books, tapes, magazines, computers, and any other relevant tools that would lead them toward the identification of men and women who could become their role models or even mentors. This "in-class" library would also contain additional media support that would encourage and inspire them to attain their best by emphasizing goal-setting, time management, communication skills, and image building.

I can remember books about famous and successful people that I read while I was in school. As I think back to the contents of many of these books, I realize that one important reality of life seemed to always be omitted—the failures along the way. If students think that life is all about succeeding every time, then failure, one of life's greatest realities, is excluded. This omission gives them a false impression of what to expect. If a student begins to dream but meets failure or failures along the way, sooner or later, he may give into one of life's biggest roadblocks. But if the books the students read are written with truth and don't try to avoid the parts of life that may not be too honorable, then true reality has become a part of the learning process. What the students would learn about failure is that it does not have to be permanent. It is only a roadblock, detour, or stepping stone to their life's achievements. Life is like an airplane that flies from New

York to Los Angeles. Changes have to be made for different air speeds, weather, or delays at the incoming airport. If it weren't for the adjustments along the way, the airplane would never land at its correct destination.

When I was a school teacher, I tried my best to include this aforementioned material. I always felt that a motivated student would always make the grade. I knew that I could teach my students how to write and speak grammatically correct, but if they passed through my class and did not leave a more motivated person, then I had failed them as their teacher. If a student doesn't know where he is going, chances are that he will probably get nowhere. The earlier a person knows where he wants to go, the better the chances are for him to achieve his dream. After my students had read and studied the lives of success-oriented individuals, I would experience the greatest thrill as a teacher when I saw that light bulb come on and heard them say, "I can do that."

When I was in school, I was always confused whenever I was assigned a topic for my term papers that had absolutely nothing to do with my interests in life. Maybe I never understood the purpose for assigning these topics. But, oh, what if I had to write a term paper about something I loved? Could it be that my passion for life could have been discovered while doing the research for my term paper?

This class was a dream that I once had for education. Although I did not get to see the fruition of this dream, somewhere in the scheme of God's plan there will be a young teacher who says, "I can do that."

He Was My Best Friend and I Miss Him

If you knew him as "Speedy," you grew up in Crowville, Louisiana. If you knew him as "Pooby," or the "little captain," you knew him at Louisiana College in Pineville, Louisiana. If you knew him as "Coach," then you met him after he began his coaching career.

When my mother was dying from cancer and going in and out of consciousness, her eyes would light up and the biggest smile would come upon her face when thoughts of Tallulah came to mind, even though she could not recall what they were. The cancer had penetrated the brain, totally obliterating specific thoughts. She just knew that the thoughts of Tallulah were about good things. Then a dark cloud would cover her demeanor when thoughts of Monroe entered her consciousness. Although she could not recall what happened in Monroe either, she said that something very bad had happened. Of course, she was referring to the death of her husband and our father, who passed away in 1958 while coaching at Northeast Louisiana State College (now ULM).

When I think of the challenges that I faced growing up trying to live up to my daddy's legacy, I realize that it is much better to live "up" to a name than to live "down" to a name. I was so proud to have a name to live up to. It was an honor. I am sixty-five years old, and my daddy's name can still open doors for my family and me.

On one occasion, while I was sitting in the waiting room at a local hospital, one of his former players came over to talk. It never takes long for one of daddy's former players to start talking about the coach whom they loved. He looked at me and said, "Robert Charles, I surely do miss your daddy."

This was the year 2004, and a player who had played for him in 1958 still missed him. I replied, "I do too."

Yes, I miss him very much. I was thirteen when he died. I miss not being able to hunt and fish with him. I regret the fact that my wife and children never got to meet him. But what I miss more than anything is not being able to talk with him and ask for his advice. Oh, to be able to ask, "Daddy, what would you have done," or "what should I do?"

If your father is alive, take advantage of his still being here. And ask all those questions that you will wish you could ask when he has gone.

Why I Don't Gamble

I wrote a column in our Sunday school's newsletter explaining why I don't gamble. The underlying principle is similar to the reason that I don't drink. It is not that I am such a righteous person that I don't drink, but I never drink because I cannot stand the stuff. And I don't gamble because I would not be very good at gambling, either. Most of the time when I go to the bank, the car wash, or the check-out line at Wal-Mart, I am reminded of why I don't gamble. I can never get in the right line no matter how short the line may look.

I was reminded of this once again when I tried to check out at Wal-Mart the other day. I had gone to Wal-Mart to buy some bird feed. Wal-Mart was about as empty as I had ever seen it. As I was walking to check out, I thought that I would swing by the flower section to buy some flowers for the two special women in my household. I had passed up several empty check-out counters, and so I thought that the extra time that it took me to go get the flowers would not delay me since the lines were very short.

After I had gotten the flowers, I picked out a line with only one man in it. Since his buggy was already packed, I thought that he would soon be on his way. I was wrong. As he was packing his merchandise in his buggy, the cashier was standing there looking bewildered. This was not a good sign. After several minutes, I noticed him pull out his check book and two credit cards—not a good sign. I have gotten behind these speed-writing champions before. By the time that he had finished writing his check, my flowers had already begun to wilt. He handed her the check, but then I noticed both of them standing there as if they were waiting for someone to tell them what to do next. I heard her tell him, "I have to get the manager for that." We waited. I thought that it had been at least thirty minutes before a lady, who would have made a good sumo wrestler, finally walked up. As long as it had taken her to come to the register, she must have been flown in from Japan. She punched a few buttons, turned a key, and left. Good sign, right? No, this was only the check-writing part. Now it was time for him to start trying his two credit cards. The cashier had to come around to the customer's side at least three times to punch buttons. Then I would hear him ask, "What does that mean?" She would tell him, and then he would say, "That's not what I wanted." But finally, all good things must come to an end. The man held a yellow legal pad that was filled with enough information to have been a handwritten Constitution. It must have been his things-to-do list. He must have completed his chores because he finally left. I looked at the cashier and said, "Must be his first time to come to town."

It's the Little Things

It is the little things that make a great big difference. A post-it note from one of your children with "you are the greatest" written on it. A little note from your spouse stuck to your pillow saying "I love you." Or maybe a little flower that someone has placed on your dresser.

When Elizabeth, our oldest granddaughter, gets to come to West Monroe for those brief visits from Jackson, every moment is precious. A visit to the zoo with her granddaddy will be etched into our memories forever. Our little talks as we walk along, looking at all the animals, will be part of our mental recordings for the days ahead. Sitting down and eating some nachos together at the lunch tables outside under the trees, we try to make up for the lost time.

Tonight, I was the recipient of one of those little things that make a great big impression. It warmed my heart and brought tears to my eyes. As I sat down to try to write something meaningful for From The Heart, I saw one of my index card folders lying on my desk in front of my computer. I did not know what it was doing there because I had not put it there. Opening it up, I saw in big orange, blue, and black letters the words, "I LOVE YOU! Granddaddy." And under the words "I love you" were even bigger letters, orange and outlined in black. There was a big "I," and then a heart with a face with eyes, nose, and big lips drawn inside the heart. The heart had hair on it like a little girl's. This picture was followed by the big letter "U."

My granddaughter needs me just like I need her. One time she said to Donna, "Granddaddy is my biggest friend." I still think she feels that way even though our visits have become brief and too far in between, but I have learned to cherish every minute with her.

Who Gave You a
Head Start in Your Life?

I have found that as I get older I do reminisce a lot more than I did in the past. I think one reason is to remind myself of how blessed I was as a child. I know there are government programs called the Head Start Programs. These programs provide the less fortunate with a more solidifying foundation to give them a chance of a more rewarding future. The program with which I was provided was a head start program; it was provided, not by the government, but by the Payne family.

A lot of the food that was provided for me was food for thought. Our family never had to worry about having enough mental food, especially the high protein created from encouragement. I don't know if we were considered poor. My mother and father both had college degrees, but we did not have much materially. Not much has changed financially for teachers. But if our family was considered poor, we did not know it. A lot of the kids that I went to school with had a lot more materially than my family had, especially at Lee Junior High and Neville High School. Nonetheless, the Payne family did not lack anything. Yes, we had our own head start program.

The greatest challenge for the Payne family was when we lost the head of our family—our father. We lost him physically, but our mother never allowed our father to die spiritually. I would consider my mother a good psychologist. Although Mother was a very intelligent and gifted person herself, she was not a braggart, for she directed our admiration and attention toward our father. Maybe it was because we were all boys and she knew that, as athletes, we would all have our athletic heroes. Athletics were so much a part of our family. (The first thing that I was given as a newborn was not a baby bottle, but a football.) Mother wanted our hero to be our father. She left Daddy's scrapbooks out on the coffee tables so that the clippings about "Speedy" Payne, the "little" captain, or the coach were there for us to admire again and again. I don't know if I have ever met anyone as unselfish or devoted as our mother. Her ego was in its proper place. Her love for her husband, our daddy, was the light that shone so brightly that it remained as our guiding light to help us through the dark spots in our lives. There is no doubt that my mother and father gave me a head start in life.

Have you ever known someone that made a statement to you that totally changed the way of your thinking? I once had a man ask me what I wanted. I told him what it was. Then he told me to go get it, and I told him that I would. I left that conversation to have the best years of my life. I think back to a time in high school when I was going through a tough sophomore year because of knee problems. During that time, Coach Bill Ruple said four words to me: "Your day will come." I think back to two words that Coach Charlie Brown said to me after our final ball game my junior year: "Thank you." There is no doubt that these few words gave me a head start for the years to come.

No matter what has happened to us and no matter the background or limitations that we have been told that we have, there is always someone there to give us a boost—a new start with a head start.

I would love for you to tell me about who gave you a head start.

Time Wasted or Time Invested

When we remember that it is the small things that make a great big difference, we should be aware that years are made of months, months are made of weeks, weeks are made of days, days are made of minutes, and minutes are made of seconds.

How valuable is your time? How well do you manage your time? Suppose I give you $86,400. The only stipulation is that you must spend the entire $86,400 within twenty-four hours of receiving the money. You cannot put it in savings. You must spend it. Whatever the amount that you have left at the end of that twenty-four hour period must be returned to me. You cannot reclaim any of the unspent money.

Now what would you do? Do you think that you would spend it all? Of course you would. No one would be so foolish as to throw away this money, but that is exactly what we do with our time. We are given 86,400 seconds everyday. How much of that time do you spend wisely? The time that you spend can never be returned to you. Time cannot be saved for another day. Wasting valuable time is just as foolish as not spending the entire $86,400.

I stated earlier that days and weeks are made of minutes. If you waste a mere thirty minutes daily, you have lost twenty-two eight-hour working days in a year. Will you allow your competitor to have twenty-two more eight-hour days to get the business? If you are wasting time, it is happening now.

Do you realize that even when you waste a mere ten minutes daily, it adds up to seven full work days in one year and 365 days over a fifty-year period? Time does not discriminate. We all have the same twenty-four hour days, and success is often the result of the way a man uses his time.

One of the best methods of time management is establishing a priority list. Make a list of things that need to be done on a daily basis. After you have made the list, rank them by priority. Number

> *"You can't throw an egg in the barnyard in the evening and expect it to be crowing by in the morning. It takes time. Be patient."*
> Cavett Robert

them one through ten or whatever. To establish the priority, you must rank them in the order in which they must be accomplished. This decision has to be made before you can begin to move forward. Put first things first. When you start the day, begin with number one. Number one must be done before you can go to number two. And two must be done before going to three and so on. Now sometimes it may be impossible because of circumstances to follow the priority list in the exact order, but the priority list will eliminate wasted motion and help you control your time. If an assignment is not completed, place it on your list for the next day, but don't ever avoid it because it is difficult. You will catch yourself pushing the tough assignment down the list every day. By always prioritizing, you will be sure that you are not procrastinating on the more challenging jobs. By making a daily planner, you can analyze the daily sheets at night or at the end of the week. The analysis of your time requires thinking, but it will lead to efficient management of your valuable time, which is the essence of life. Motivational speaker Cavett Roberts said that if you always do what you have always done, you will always get what you always got.

So You Think You Want to Run for Public Office?

"I think that everyone should run for public office at least once."

"Yeah, and they should have to serve for six months whether they win or lose."

This was a conversation I had with the former mayor of West Monroe, Bert Hatten, shortly after I had run for state representative in 1982. Running for state representative was one of the most demanding challenges that I had ever faced. My wife, other family members, a few friends, and some church folks who believed in our mission were all that we had. We worked tirelessly up until the final night of the election. Donna was there by my side from start to finish. All we knew how to do was work and ask for votes. And when it was all said and done, one of the state's most colorful politicians said to me, "Robert Charles, the pros win. Amateurs come close."

As one of the amateurs who came close, I would like to share some campaign stories from 1982. If we learned one thing, it was that you must learn to be humorous, because at times all you can do is just laugh. Your skin must be as thick as that of a pachyderm.

When I first entered the race, I had no clue what to do, especially how to run a campaign without any money. Thinking that I should call on someone who knew politics, I went over to the Chateau Restaurant to have lunch with Mr. Joe Cascio. He told me to find out who was number one in the race and beat on him. I tracked down the latest poll to find out who it was. Guess what? It was me! And yes, Mr. Cascio was right: I was severely beat upon. I learned that it is much better to start out as number two or even three, so that you can fly under the radar unnoticed until you can make your serious charge.

One day, a senior citizen asked to which party I belonged. Now you must understand that in 1982 it was not politically correct to be a Republican. I really did not know the difference between a Republican, Democrat, or an Independent, but my party affiliation cost me dearly. Now back to the story. The elderly lady was determined to find my party affiliation. Since senior citizens did not look upon Republicans favorably, I was trying to ignore her question. When she persisted, I told her that I was an American. Because she was not satisfied with that, I finally told her that I was a Republican. She yelled at me, "You caused the Depression." To which I replied, "Lady, I was not even born then."

One of the more serious allegations that I faced was running rampant at the mill. One gentleman who had heard these rumors wanted me to confirm or deny these allegations. I said, "Sir, what is it?" He answered in quite a serious tone, "There is a rumor running throughout the mill that you don't like to dog hunt. Is that true?"

Then on another occasion, one politician told me that I was getting a lot of criticism because I was one of those "reborn" Christians. I think that he meant "born again."

If you are considering a "run for the roses," then I encourage you to "go for it." You may be a David going against the Goliaths, but remember that David won. That is what is so great about America. Sometimes, the amateurs do win.

Would You Chase Your Dream for Forty-Five Years?

I love the Bible story of Caleb. Caleb's story is about a man who was promised his mountain at forty years of age but did not receive it until he was eighty-five. How many of us would wait forty-five years for our mountain? How many of us could endure forty-five years of perseverance? *Webster's Unabridged Dictionary* defines *perseverance* as follows: "steady persistence in a course of action, a purpose, a state, especially in spite of difficulties, obstacles, or discouragement." Caleb was one of the greatest mountain climbers in the history of mankind. And what an optimist! When he and a few others were sent to scout the enemy for their king, all of them except Caleb said that the obstacles in their path were too big. The enemies were giants and the walls were too high. Caleb told the king that they could win the battle: "All we have to do is believe in our purpose!"

One of the greatest difficulties in reaching our dreams is that we quit too quickly. Life has a way of testing us when we are very close to fulfilling our dreams. Usually the greatest challenge that we will face is immediately before the manifestation of our dream. Sometimes this obstacle is of monumental proportions. Add this latest discouragement to the other delays, detours, and failures that we have faced along the way, and we ask ourselves, "Is it worth it?"

Most of us would "throw in the towel" if we had to wait forty-five years to see the completion of our dream. Can you imagine the perseverance that was required? Caleb never wavered about claiming his dream, his mountain. He had the same belief about acquiring his dream at eighty-five that he had when he was forty. Most of us panic when the years begin to pile up on us. These are the thoughts that follow us as we age:

"Forty is young, and there is plenty of time for me to reach my goals."

"Fifty. It is still not too late, but something had better happen soon."

When we reach that traumatic age of sixty and still have not arrived, this discouragement leads to depression. "Oh, what is the use?"

Then we reach seventy, and there is still no dream. Eighty arrived, still without the dream, but Caleb never quit believing in his dream. He had seen his mountain forty years ago. He had claimed his mountain forty years ago. Now at eighty-five, Caleb could feel the emotion of walking on his mountain, but at that moment in time came his greatest challenge yet—he had to conquer a land of giants in order to reach his mountain. Nevertheless, he was strong, alert, healthy, and ready. He deserved this mountain. It had been promised to him forty-five years earlier. Finally, he won his battles, overcoming all obstacles and conquering the last barriers. He had remained focused for forty-five years and now was walking on his own mountain. What a great example of perseverance!

What did it take for Caleb to get to his mountain? First, he had to believe in his dreams and the God who promised him his mountain. Second, he had to overcome the giants who were in his way. (What giants in your life have made you afraid? Who have been the giant dream killers?) Third, Caleb never changed his focus. He kept his eyes on his mountain. (Have you lost your focus? It is never too late to regain your focus.) The last characteristic Caleb portrayed was perseverance. He never quit, and at eighty-five years of age, Caleb walked on his mountain.

It is never too late.

Sharing Lessons of a Lifetime

I have come to the realization that I am not the sharpest knife in the kitchen when it comes to learning the rules of life. Even though I have been a slow learner, here are twenty-five simple rules for living that I did learn along the way of this most interesting journey that we call life.

1. "There is a God, and I'm not Him."—Quote by a Catholic priest in the movie *Rudy*
2. When your light goes out, the bugs go away.
3. Trying to change others is like throwing marshmallows at a mountain, so work on yourself.
4. The sun is always shining, no matter what.
5. Hold me; don't scold me.
6. I was always afraid of failure until I failed, and I had to learn to adjust and try again, or I would die.
7. The only difference between a giant and an ant is quite small—only two letters.
8. There is no greater blessing than for a teacher to help students recognize their talents.
9. Character is what we are when nobody is watching.
10. The most important learning center that we have for children is found at the center of family.
11. Forgiveness is not a choice. If you want to continue to live, forgiveness is mandatory.
12. Tragedy is the fire that burns you pure or burns you up.
13. "One can not govern with buts."—Charles de Gaulle "Nor can one govern with butts."—Robert Charles Payne
14. My scars taught me to look up at the stars. Before my scar, I was the star, because I had no sight.
15. Too much knowledge or too much wine gives the same result.

16. You don't know what real living is until you have lost what you love.
17. As you get much older, your secrets are safe with your old friends. They can't remember them.
18. If you want to see the sunrise, you must wake up in the dark.
19. It is easy to forgive when you are having a good day.
20. There is no life without relationships.
21. As teachers, what we say is not nearly as important as what the student remembers.
22. Blaming others is like getting angry because your shoes are laced too tight.
23. "If a man does his best, what else is there?"
    —George Patton
24. It is better to be alone than in bad company.
25. The future belongs to those who believe in the beauty of their dreams.

I have written and collected power phrases most of my life. Some are my own that came to me after I had learned a valuable lesson through a life experience. Our life experiences filter our thoughts, and our perceptions are the result of this filter. Some perceptions are unique, but most thoughts are universal because we all live through the cycle of life. Some lives are shorter than others, but life is a journey—a school of testing, learning, growing, failing, rebounding, and developing our doctrine of beliefs that are used as building blocks or stumbling blocks. How we react to the events in our lives determines how we stand or how we fall. Life is all about choices. But I do agree with General George Patton: "If a man does his best, what else is there?"

Toe-Tapping,
Hand-Clapping Good Time

Wow! Wow! Wow! What a great time we had at the fundraiser held for the flood victims at the Pentecostal Church in West Monroe. This was the first time that I had been in their beautiful new sanctuary. There is not a bad seat in the house. I know that Brother Mark Foster and his church members are very proud of their new facilities. Sunday night, all the visitors were greeted with a big smile and a warm handshake.

After all of us had settled into our seats, we watched the countdown on the big screens. If we had not been in church, I don't think that we all would have counted down to lift off. There was not one person who left there that did not feel better than when he walked in. It made no difference if you were Baptist, Methodist, Presbyterian, Pentecostal, Episcopalian, Church of God, or Catholic nor what doctrine was represented—there was only one big heart Sunday night.

Starting with congregational singing led by the worship leader and the praise team of the Pentecostal Church, all hearts were prepared for a night filled with hope for the future and gratitude for all the blessings of life. The pastor from New Orleans, whose church and home were both under water, expressed that no matter what, "we are blessed." When the evacuees were recognized, I could only imagine the challenges and hardships that they had faced and that they would be facing. We were reminded that, even though the airways have been filled with the news about the flood and its victims, we should not forget all the victims when all the news coverage goes away, because they will still be living with the trials of a long recovery.

Judge Wendell Manning shared some of his experiences with the Red Cross. He mentioned people and said that when he saw each of their faces, he saw the face of Christ. Judge, we heard the message.

A lot of toe-taps, hand-claps, big smiles, and warm hearts joined each group as they entertained with the enthusiasm of an old time revival. Sonny Franks and the Chordsmen were the first group. I still don't see how Sonny's voice gets so high. The Pacemakers (now the River City Quartet, Judge William Norris, Mayor Dave Norris, Sonny Franks, and Bill Welch) sang next. The mayor's wife, Biddy, has been playing the piano for them for all these years. The judge touched all of us when he sang "How Great Thou Art." Donna has always told me that she thought the Pacemakers were better than those quartets on television. We were also blessed to hear our own highly successful husband and wife team now living in Nashville—the Hemphills. One of the songs they sang was a song that Joel had written himself, "The Master of the Wind." Our mayor and his family added another big wow. What a talented family! And I figured out last night why I did not get elected to a political office— I can't sing.

Never Give Up

"When things go wrong, as they sometimes will, when the road you're trudging seems all uphill," never give up. Have you ever felt like this? These are the first two lines of the poem "Don't Quit." The author is unknown, but you can tell he had been down some rough roads.

He knew what it felt like "when the funds are low and the debts are high." Have you ever owed more than you can repay? "And you want to smile, but you have to sigh"? This is the thought that you have when you feel as if the world has passed you by and "when care is pressing down a bit."

The Bible says that the cares of this world choke the Word in you. Your worries create anxieties that keep you from reaching your potential. "Rest, if you must, but don't you quit" is such good advice. Take a break. Stop. Regroup. Rest. "Life is queer with its twists and turns, as every one of us sometimes learns." All of us can identify with this line: "And many a failure turns about, when he might have won had he stuck it out." The world is full of people who gave up and "threw in the towel." "Don't give up, though the pace seems slow." Persistence is the key to overcoming all odds. "You may succeed with another blow" if you had tried only one more time. "Often the goal is nearer than it seems to a faint and faltering man."

Vince Lombardi said that fatigue makes cowards of us all. I think fear causes us to shrink when we ought to be growing. "Often the struggler

> "I don't know the key to success, but the key to failure is trying to please everybody."
>
> Bill Cosby

has given up, when he might have captured the victor's cup. And he learned too late when night slipped down. How close he was to the golden crown." Oh, how many of us have thought what might have been if we had only not quit. When Germany was about to overtake Great Britain during World War II, Winston Churchill shouted these words to British Parliament: "Never, never, never, never, never, give up." It was one of the most powerful speeches ever delivered, and it was only seven words long. "Success is failure turned inside out."

I have heard some extremely successful people who have always identified problems as opportunities. "The silver tint of the clouds of doubt." Doubt cripples belief. "And you never can tell how close you are. It might be near when it seems so far." The world has a way of testing you by trying to discourage you right before your dreams come true. "So stick to the fight when you're hardest hit." It is so hard to recover sometimes, especially when the hit was a knock-out punch and your mind is cloudy and your legs are weak. "It's when things seem worst that you must not quit." You must try one more time.

Abraham Lincoln was knocked down many times, but he kept getting back up one more time and eventually became the president of the United States. Sylvester Stallone's manuscript for *Rocky* was rejected over thirty times, but he sent it in one more time. My own father was rejected by one college because he was too small, and so he hitchhiked to another college where he became an All-American. Vince Lombardi, the famous coach of the Green Bay Packers, was told that he did not know enough football and could not motivate either, but he did not listen to the experts.

These people never quit, and they kept trying until their dreams came true.

It Is Well with My Soul

When I taught high school English, I always had my students research the life of the author of whatever work we might be studying. I wanted them to be aware of the history behind the work and of what had influenced the author's thoughts. I wanted them to know that there was a story behind every poem, every novel, every song, and every written book.

The words in many great works were written out of a broken heart. Horatio G. Spafford, an extremely successful businessman, wrote the words to the song "It Is Well with My Soul" in 1873. His family life had been doing as well as his business life. Then the first of several misfortunes struck him and his wife, Anna. In 1871, they lost their baby boy. This was the beginning of several tragedies. In 1873, the Chicago fire totally wiped out all of his real estate and business holdings.

After spending time trying to regroup from this terrible tragedy, Spafford decided to purchase six tickets for his four young daughters, his wife, and himself on the huge ocean liner, the *Ville Du Havre*. He was going to move his family from Chicago so they could break away from these dark memories. The night before he and his family were to leave on the voyage, Spafford was called into some business meetings that were related to the fire. Since he would not be able to miss the meetings that were to take place over the next several days, he sent his wife and four children ahead on the *Ville Du Havre*. He would board another ship within the next few days and meet them later in England. Four days into the voyage, the *Ville Du Havre* was broad-sided by another ocean liner and sank. His four daughters perished, and his wife sent him a telegram that read, "I alone saved."

Spafford boarded a ship the next day and sailed to England to meet his wife. Several days into his voyage, the captain of the vessel told Horatio that they would soon be in the area where the *Ville Du Havre* went down. As Spafford sat there alone in his cabin, a torrent of emotions began to overflow him the very moment his ship was passing over the spot where the *Ville Du Havre* sank. From this emotional surge, he pinned the words to "It Is Well with My Soul."

Spafford once said, "I am glad to trust the Lord when it will cost something." His statement made me think about how I responded to my own misfortunes down through the years. I wish that I, too, could make the same statement Spafford made. However, I have found that faith and forgiveness are easy to proclaim when things are going well.

On November 22, 1875, Philip Bliss wrote the music to Horatio Spafford's poem, "It Is Well with My Soul." This song is considered one of the top five hymns ever to be written in America. Every great song, novel, poem, play, or speech was usually sparked by a time of suffering when the author was able to transfer his thoughts from his heart through his pen into his written words.

"When peace like a river" flows through the tributaries of our hearts, then we can rest in stillness because it is well with our souls.

The Joy of Discovering the Mysteries of the Universe

This morning when I walked out to get the paper, the first thing I recognized was the coolness in the air. I love the coolness, but not the coldness. Coldness causes me to be more concerned with keeping warm than with enjoying where I am and what is around me. As soon as I stepped out the door this morning, I was met with cool kisses to my nose and cheeks. When morning greets me in this manner, I immediately breathe in this newness. I feel so alive. I feel welcomed by the new season, almost as if I am embraced by a friend who has shared much of life with me. When I look up and see the crystal clear sky full of stars, there is a reawakening of so many good memories.

This morning sky stirred thoughts of deer hunting. I have observed many starlit skies while hunting. I liked getting on my stand very early, not necessarily for the hunt, but to just sit and be amazed. I was captivated by the sheer beauty above me. I was awestruck by the speed of the shooting stars. I wished that I knew more about the constellations so I could search them out from my deer stand. I thought that I had observed quite a few starry skies of nights that were so clear that the Milky Way stood out like glittering sand for as far as I could see.

One year, my brother Andy and I took two of our sons to southwest Texas for a deer hunt. Since I was no longer deer hunting at this time, I went to sit on my stand to enjoy the works of the Master Artist. This trip introduced me to a part of the universe that I had never been able to see before. We were so far away from the city lights that you could see from horizon to horizon. Nothing blocked your view.

I could not believe the magnificent splendor of the southwest Texas sky. It took my breath away. This sky made me feel like a little boy in an observatory. There wasn't a spot in the black sky where there weren't stars at some depth. I could see the movements of ten or twelve airplanes traveling in all directions.

After the morning hunts, I could not wait to return that evening to watch the late afternoon color change into a magical kingdom of stars. I felt embraced by my Creator. To know that I am only a speck—not even a speck in this universe—and still be important made me feel loved. My mind could not grasp what was before me. To try to comprehend the thought that the universe I could see could be fitted upon the head of a pin in comparison to the incomprehensible size of other universes was mind-boggling.

But you know what excited me even more? To know how much more to life there is. Many of the things in life that I feel are so important are like shadows that disappear when the sun is masked behind the clouds. Yes, there is so much to learn and so much to enjoy.

Some worry about getting bored with life, especially after retirement, but it is the mysteries of God's ways that make life exciting and livable. And He allows His children the freedom to find the secrets and the joy that accompanies these discoveries.

A Very Exciting Late-Night Phone Call

Donna and I had been married for almost one week when we received a late night telephone call. I expected it to be one of those phone calls from someone wanting the funeral home. Our new telephone number had been the former number of a funeral home—lucky us. (It did not take me long to get our number changed.) However, this call was one of the most exciting calls that I had ever received in my lifetime. At this point in my life, I was playing semi-pro football for the Twin City Panthers, which had been formed two years earlier. The call was from an assistant coach from a team in the Canadian Football League. He introduced himself and then asked if I would like to come play for them. I did not hesitate to answer him with a resounding, "Yes!"

I had spent the past four years trying to get a shot at playing professional football and had become my own PR man. I had put together a scrapbook of my playing days at Northeast Louisiana State College (now ULM). I had written every team in the NFL trying to get a tryout. Since I had not finished playing out my college eligibility, I had to promote myself. I had had a coach that did not have the same philosophy about football as my daddy and my high school coach had. Since I had always had a dream of getting a chance to play in the NFL, when the Twin City Panthers was formed, I jumped at the chance to play again.

When I received that midnight phone call, it looked as if my dreams of playing professional football were still alive. The coach on the other end of the line asked me how much money I wanted. Wow! How much money did I want? I just wanted to play. I had never even thought about playing for money. I told him that I needed to talk it over with my agent. You know that I am kidding. The only agent that I had was my insurance agent. I would have played for nothing. Anyway, we discussed the contract further, and then he told me that he would send the contract in the mail. I could sign it and send it back. He said that all the information about training camp would be included in the package.

Donna had overheard the conversation, but she was not sure what was going on or to whom I was talking. When I hung up, she asked me who had been on the phone, and I told her that it was a coach from the Canadian Football League who wanted me to play for them. Then she asked me which team he coached. Guess what? In all the excitement, I had completely forgotten. Can you imagine that I finally got the opportunity of my life and had forgotten which team he coached? No matter how hard I tried to recall the team, I could not remember. Laying my head back down on the pillow, I put my arms around my new bride and said, "Boy, I sure hope he calls back."

Well, he did not call back, but two weeks later, the contract from the Winnipeg Blue Bombers came in the mail. I will not tell you the amount of the contract that I signed, but it was for much more than I was making as an assistant coach at Lee Junior High School.

How Often Do You Go to the Movies?

When is the last time you went to the movies? Some may go once or twice a month. Some people go every Friday night. Some may say that they don't go at all. But no matter what your answer is, we actually go to the movies every day of our lives.

I don't know how many are aware of these movies, but we are always watching the movies that are constantly running in our minds. These movies have the greatest influence upon our lives whether we are aware of it or not.

Our minds are like a Polaroid camera. The object of the camera is like a new idea. Only a few minutes after the picture is taken, the figures that were in the camera's eye begin to manifest. In the

> "We must be the change we want to see in the world."
> Gandhi

end, we have a clear picture in the photograph. Those objects seen through the camera lenses are now manifested. It is the same with the mind. Whatever you watch in your mind long enough begins to manifest into real objects.

We don't like to admit sometimes that maybe we are to blame for some of our problems, but those who are aware of the influence of their thoughts usually have better outcomes. I know some will take offense to this statement. Even I would like to take offense, but many of the outcomes in my life are the result of my thinking. There are some things in my life that I don't have a clue why they happened, but I am aware that the way I think is highly influential on the outcome.

For the readers who are deer hunters sitting there on those most frigid mornings, usually freezing to death, once those footsteps are heard out there somewhere, you forget about how cold it is. You are completely warm while listening and waiting for that big buck to stick his head out. But the minute those steps go out of range, you remember that you are freezing.

The same scenario takes place while duck hunting. There can be ice on the water and that cold wind biting you in the face, but once the ducks start flying and the caps start popping, thoughts of the weather disappear until all the excitement has died down.

Have you ever been to an athletic event, such as a football game, when a team is behind four touchdowns? Then it seems as if a brand new team has taken the field and momentum has swung toward the team that is losing. The losing team rallies for five touchdowns in one quarter. What do you think happens? Do you think all of a sudden the team that is behind has developed more talent in a matter of minutes? No. There is a mental shift. The focus on their thoughts of losing the game has become reality. The thoughts of a deadline drawing near take over, and miraculously, there seems to be a new team on the field. Was it a miraculous physical transformation? Not at all. They had the same physical ability that they had at the beginning of the game. The transformation was mental. Those mental movies of the possibility of losing the game became such a driving force that those wires of nerves that feed the muscular and skeletal systems went into overdrive and a metamorphosis took place. A new mindset occurred. Yes, you really do become what you think about.

Education and Reality Shows

The most popular shows on television today are the reality shows. Our educational classrooms should be reality shows. If our classrooms would become more of a reality of making the students aware of why these subjects are important in their lives, then the purpose of the subjects would become clearer. Most of the questions from students about why the subjects are needed are usually answered with generic statements: "They are part of the curriculum" or "You will need them."

I was watching a television special on LPB the other night. They were interviewing a student who had begun to cause trouble in school. He had been making D's and F's and was ready to drop out of school. He explained what happened when he was transferred to another curriculum and had a class under a new teacher. This teacher was able to show the student why his assignments were applicable to real life. Once the student became aware of why the subject was applicable to his life, his grades catapulted to almost all A's. Did the student suddenly become smarter? Did his intelligence increase because he was now a few months older and his brain had grown? Of course not.

He had become aware of why the subject was relative. His assignments were applicable, and he could correlate between what he had learned in the classroom and his own life. This relevance between subject and life stirred his passion for learning. His sleeping giant within was awakened. He was motivated toward achievement, not only because he wanted to make good grades, but also because he had become aware of the importance of the subject. This newfound awareness stirred this inner desire that released his hidden abilities. From this revelation, he began to use his gifts. Because his passions had been stirred, good grades became a by-product of his desire to learn and his desire to apply what he had learned. School had become important because it had become relative to his own life.

I spent my entire educational career trying to get the educational establishment to understand what motivates students to learn. I have a three-ring binder full of letters that I had received from educational leaders, both state and national, after I had written them about my classroom. They would congratulate me and tell me to keep up the good work. However, I did not need them to tell me to keep up the good work. I needed them to publicly promote education and the teachers who made a difference, an action that requires leadership. The problem that progressive teachers face is that many educational leaders are interested in keeping the status quo alive and standardized test scores up. They are not interested in anything that will require adjustment and change. Most positions that are political appointments do not require leadership. Education needs a leader.

It should be a required mission statement of each classroom to make the student aware of the purpose of the subject. Why is this subject taught? How is it relative to the student's life? As the class progresses, the student should be able to apply what he has learned as a building block toward the accomplishment of his personal dreams and goals.

Laughter Is the Best Medicine

Laughter is the best medicine. Norman Cousins proved how true this statement is when he was healed of a terminal illness by heavy doses of laughter. In his book, *Anatomy of an Illness*, Cousins tells how he was healed by watching hours of humorous movies. I thought that this certainly

> *"Enjoy the little things, for one day you will look back and discover they were the big things."*
> Author Unknown

would be a good place for me to start my own healing, and so I bought some old DVDs of Jack Benny, Lucille Ball, and Milton Beryl. Just plain, simple comedy. I am going to try to share a few true stories that I hope will bring a chuckle or even a deep belly laugh. Maybe your laughter will be the start of your own healing process.

Football players and Tallulah, Louisiana, provided several of these stories. When we lived in Tallulah, we had an English bulldog named Bubbles. One afternoon, Daddy had Bubbles with him at the football stadium. One of his players had come by and was talking to my Daddy when he said, "Coach Payne, I believe that is the ugliest dog I have ever seen." After laughing about the remark, they continued with their visiting. I am sure that the young man had forgotten about his earlier remark when he told his coach, "You know, Coach Payne, that dog looks a lot like you."

Then one night during a football game, one of Daddy's players was injured. Daddy was running out to check on the player when the injured player's mother appeared out of nowhere, bent over her son, and loudly asked him, "Henry, are you hurt or are you just drunk again?"

Joe Driskell, a former player during the old Northeast Louisiana State College era, was one of the college's first professional football players. He played for the St. Louis Cardinals. Joe was always one of my all-time favorites among Daddy's former players. He shared this story with me. He told me that the team was watching films one day and Daddy kept running the same play over and over. He would run it, then reverse it, and run it, and reverse it again. Joe said that he did this about ten times and then made a comment to one of the players. "Robert, it does not matter how many times I keep running this play back; you miss your block every time." Joe loved to tell me stories about Coach Payne. We lost this great American soldier and athlete several years ago. He had made a career out of the service and had risen to the rank of general. Like his cousin said at the memorial service, "Joe was my hero."

My insurance career provided the material for this next story. A lady called in one day to insure a pleasure boat, or what we call a party barge. When I was getting the information from her, I asked her if it was a party barge. She quickly answered, "Oh, no. We don't drink. We are Christians."

If your family is like mine, there is a lot of visiting going on at the dinner table. In fact, some of my children's friends have remarked that they have never had so much fun eating in their lives. They said all they did was laugh. One day when my daughter Laurie was about four or five, she said, "Daddy, I can spell pizza."

"You can. Let me hear you spell pizza."

To which she excitedly began to spell, "J-O-H-N-N-Y-S." Did Johnny Huntsman, the founder of a pizza franchise, have influence on our kids, or what?

Now get well, stay healthy, and laugh a lot.

Walking Is More Than Exercise

I get so much done when I walk each day. Not only do I get my physical exercise but, much more than that, I also get my mental and my spiritual exercise. I try to walk every day for at least forty-five minutes to an hour. This daily exercise is an important part in the healing process of my cancer. Every time I inhale, I take in life, and each breath I exhale, I am a giver of life. Our health and well-being are based upon balance. For every cause, there is an effect.

I learned to write while I was walking so that I could record the ideas that were birthed while I walk along my concrete path. My brain gets its exercise from the thoughts generated from the CDs I listen to and also from the sights my eyes are so privileged to see. My spirit gets its exercise from the beauty and sounds of nature.

This past evening as I walked, the descending sun burned in its bright evening orange, and the fingers from its rays touched all that was around me. Every tree had a dark outline, a shadow of its trunk and its limbs, and the leaves with the perfect timing of nature declared the season. As I looked heavenward at blue backgrounds spotted with clouds, a sense of well-being and health wrapped my body with the energy of life. Oh, how I enjoy my walks. They have become an exciting adventure.

As stated earlier, I listen to a CD while I walk. I carry a notepad so that I will not miss any ideas or thoughts that are birthed while I am walking, whether inspired by the voices from the CDs or from the sights of nature. People wonder what they can do when they retire, or what they can do as they begin to reach the ages of 60, 70, 80, and above. One thing that any of us can do, no matter our age, is to keep our thinking processes alive through whatever method we use for inspiration.

To spend time thinking while I am walking does several things. It keeps me mentally alert. It gives me the ability to create the objects of my own little universe. My walks always seem short, no matter what is on the CD, so that the time and weather does not seem to have an influence upon me. Each day, my walks become new journeys that create an inner excitement, adding joy and more purpose for living.

A little more than a year ago, I was diagnosed with cancer. I knew that if I were going to live, I had to change. A crisis forces us to let go of old behaviors. When my wife was diagnosed with breast cancer four years ago, our lives changed. From the very moment you hear the words, "We found cancer," your life will never be the same.

Donna and I changed. Our marriage changed. What was important to us changed. And now, once again, cancer has raised its ugly head. When my daughter, Laurie, saw me after learning that I had cancer, she said, "We beat it once with Momma's. We will beat it again."

Everyday, I walk to live. For those of you who may one day hear these same words, "You have cancer," just keep in mind that cancer does not have to be a death sentence.

Remember Those Classic Remarks

While I was a junior at Neville High School, my team played Ouachita High School. I was on the sidelines with my shoulder in a sling from a broken collarbone, but a classic remark was made that night by one of my teammates.

We had scored on three straight punt returns. After the third straight return for a TD, Nickie White, a tremendous defensive player as well as a genius when it came to knowing what to do on the field, remarked to Coach Charlie Brown, "Coach Brown, if you will keep your offense off the field, we will run up the score for you." The offense had not even been on the field yet, and we were ahead 21 to 0. Of course, Nickie was one of only a few that could get away with a statement like that. Nickie White was quite a story himself, a two year All-Stater, but not built like any other athlete I know. He looked more like an overweight Lou Holtz than a linebacker.

Coach Vann Leigh, the former long-time coach at Lee Junior High School, related this story to me years ago. He said that he had just finished giving a rousing speech and pep talk during a half-time when one of his players raised his hand to ask a question. He asked the player what he wanted. The young boy replied, "Coach Leigh, do you think dogs have dreams?" True story. Only those who have been around Coach Leigh can guess at his response.

When I was coaching at Claiborne Christian School, we had a chance at the play-offs, which would have been the first time that Claiborne had made the play-offs. We had a long shot with only one game remaining—against a team that was much more talented than we were. When we were walking into their stadium, we saw several KKK members dressed in their full regalia, because our team had several black players. Our white players just closed ranks around the young men that this display was meant to intimidate.

We were able to play within a touchdown until two of our players went down with injuries. This group of young men had faced adversity all year and had overcome it all, but this night seemed more like a bad dream. When we were traveling home, the bus was very quiet, each player deep in his own thoughts about all that had happened in the game, when one of our black players broke the silence by sharing, "Coach Payne, I have played in a lot of important games in front of a lot of people. I have played in the state championships at the Dome. But Coach Payne, I have never played in front of the Ku Klux Klan." Everyone on that bus fell out laughing. From that moment on, we all put things into proper perspective.

My daughter, Laurie, took pride in her spelling when she was a little girl. Although it would be several years before she would start school, she loved to share some of the words that she had learned to spell. One day, she told me that she could spell blue jeans. I certainly was impressed that my little daughter, only three or four years old at the time, already knew how to spell blue jeans.

"Ok, honey, let me hear you spell blue jeans."

She quickly sounded the letters, "L-E-E."

When you hear a classic, write it down.

Man's Best Friend

My wife and I make a trip to Arlington, Texas, every four months for her breast cancer check-up. When all the medical tests are complete, we spend time shopping—for Donna. We always stop at a certain pet store to view all of the new animals.

On one occasion, Donna spotted a little poodle named Pierre. When we first saw him, he looked like a big ball of cotton with two little black spots for eyes. Because Donna wanted a closer look, Pierre was brought out to an area where you could visit with the dogs. This ball of fur went round and round and then jumped up on his two little back feet, which you could not even see. How could it be that this little dog to whom you immediately became attached had not been sold? I told Donna that no one would buy him because he was a French poodle and all of America was mad at the French because of their lack of commitment in helping the United States in the war on terrorism.

Donna fell in love with him immediately. However, I told Donna that I was not going to pay that much for a dog, even if he did have a mustache. We walked out of the store without the adorable and likeable little dog named Pierre.

Several weeks later, Donna met me at our back door. She was smiling from ear to ear and could not contain her excitement. She had called the pet store and found that Pierre had not been sold and that the price had dropped considerably. Since Dylan, our nephew who lives in Dallas, was coming to Shreveport, Donna said that Dylan could bring Pierre with him. I never let Donna know, but I wanted Pierre as badly as she did. This little pooch grabbed your heart as soon as you saw him.

Pierre has brought a refreshing joy to the Payne household. This little cotton ball captures the heart of everyone who comes to our house. The way Pierre greets someone visiting our house makes that person feel as if he is the most important person in the world.

Pierre has never learned that he is a dog. He is spoiled and wants all of our attention. As soon as you walk into the house, he runs to get one of his toys, brings it to you, and expects you to throw it for him to retrieve. Furthermore, this four-legged entertainer runs through the house, sliding on the wood floors and jumping from carpet to carpet. If you don't pay attention to him, he will punch you with his nose or hit you with his two front paws.

Our little poodle loves to play and watch TV. He will chase the light of a flashlight until he is completely exhausted. He also chases squirrels and anything else that moves or makes a reflection. Sometimes it is hard to get him to use the bathroom at night because he is trying to run down the armadillo.

Oh, how he loves his Momma Donna. When she leaves the house, he whines, runs from door to door and from window to window, and finally goes into mourning on his pillow in his chair.

I have liked all my dogs, but this little friend who enthusiastically greets me every single time that I come home has won over my heart. Maybe we spouses and parents could learn a lesson from our furry friends.

What Happened to Your Dreams?

What happened to the dreams you had when you were young? Did you meet any dream killers along the way? Whom did you meet that tried to quench your spirit? Or did you meet those that stirred the gifts within you? Who were your dream makers?

I heard a visiting minister at my youngest son's church preach on this subject of dream killers and dream makers. He shared the experiences of his own life. He had a teacher who humiliated and scolded him in front of his classmates when he was in the seventh grade. The teacher told him that he would never amount to anything. This remark embarrassed him so much that he dropped out of school that day. Actually, he not only quit school, but he also quit trying. His spirit had been quenched. Because he did not think much of himself and no longer had plans for his future, he wandered for several years, confused and disappointed. The minister told us that he never stayed with a job very long.

One day, he came to a company that required him to take a psychological evaluation before he could apply for a job. When he was called in to discuss the results of the test, the psychologist informed him that he could not work for this company, because he had scored too high on the test. The test had determined that he was over-qualified. The psychologist said to him, "Son, you are too big for this job. You made the highest score that has ever been made. You need to seek a job that will allow you to use your intelligence. You have the ability to become successful at a very high level."

This young man had just met a dream maker. The psychologist had stirred the gifts within him. When he walked out of the psychologist's office that day, he had once again become a young man with a desire to dream big dreams.

Now, over thirty years later, this same young man, who had been told by his teacher that he would not amount to anything, has become an internationally known minister and evangelist. He has pastored several churches that started with only a few members and grew to become successful fellowships. He has traveled millions of miles all over the world, ministering to hundreds of thousands in almost every country on this big globe. He has shared his expertise concerning the creation of cell groups for internationally known church organizations and churches. He is the author of five books. He has influenced many young men and women to become ministers, evangelists, and missionaries. One of those he influenced is my own son, Beck, who is the youth pastor at Family Church in West Monroe, Louisiana.

For every dream that you have, you will have a dream killer, or a quencher of the spirit. However, to prevent dream killers from destroying your dreams, there is also a dream maker ready to stir the gifts within you. Reverend Billy Hornsby was that young seventh grader who was told by his teacher that he would not amount to anything. Now Brother Hornsby has become one of the world's biggest dream makers.

Who has been the driving force in your life? A dream killer or a dream maker?

Notre Dame, Oklahoma, or Northeast?

When I was about eleven years old, I loved Notre Dame and Oklahoma. I waited each year for the big battle between these two juggernauts. One of them would usually become the National Champions in collegiate football. At this time, my father was the head coach of Northeast Louisiana State College.

My Daddy and I were in a sporting goods store in Alexandria, Louisiana, visiting the owner Ransom Cole. My daddy and Ransom had been good friends for a long time. Ransom always called on the coaches all over north and central Louisiana to sell them their athletic equipment. During this particular visit, Ransom asked me where I wanted to go to college.

I proudly spoke up, "Notre Dame or Oklahoma!"

My daddy counteracted with this remark, "What do you mean 'Notre Dame or Oklahoma'? Boy, if you are any good, you will be going to Northeast. If you are not any good, you can go to Notre Dame or Oklahoma."

Ransom never let me forget that incident. I did go to Northeast, not because I had turned down offers from Notre Dame and Oklahoma, but because Northeast was the only school that offered me a scholarship. (I did not get the opportunity to play for my dad because he had passed away in 1958 when I was in the eighth grade.) I don't believe that I would have been offered a scholarship by Northeast either if Coach Jim Coates, the backfield coach, had not believed in me so much. Not many wanted this 5'8" and 155-pound big bruiser with lightning quick speed who also had broken his collarbone after only the sixth game.

Coach Coates had watched me play against Bastrop my senior year, and he told me that after that night he knew I could start as a freshman the very next year. In fact, the day that I broke my collarbone, the Northeast coaches were there checking on me. You would have thought that I was being heavily recruited based on the interest the Northeast coaches showed in me. As a young man, I did not know that I "had it so good."

Coach Coates was my position coach the next year. I don't think we had "coordinators" back then. There were not enough coaches to specialize. Everybody had to do everything.

We had used the terminology "gee" and "haw" to determine if the formation was to the left or right. One week, we were practicing for Louisiana Tech. While we were in the huddle, the quarterback called a "haw" formation. I really had struggled with the terminology all year. Usually you use words that begin with either "R" or "L" for the right or left, but I had stayed focused on these words all year. So far I had made it through the year without lining up in the wrong place, but on this day during practice, I went to the wrong side when a "gee" formation was called.

Coach Coates hollered at me, "Robert Charles, you are lined up on the wrong side. Don't you know what 'gee' means?"

"No, sir. I don't even know what 'haw' means."

You see, not many of us Neville boys had ever driven a wagon or plowed behind any mules. So, coaches, make sure that, when you select the terminology for your offense or defense, your players know what you are talking about.

Cold Days and Good Memories

The cold winter days remind me of all the years of hunting. When our daddy was the head football coach at Tallulah High School, Devone and I hunted for squirrels and deer with him in the large woods of the Madison and Tensas Parishes. We had access to some of the best hunting land in Louisiana—one of the coaching perks that we shared with our daddy.

We walked all over those big woods. There were no four-wheel drive vehicles, three-wheelers, four-wheelers, or six-wheelers. People had tractors. Some had an old army jeep. There were some of those international trucks that had some type of special engine that allowed them to travel where other trucks could not. Therefore, once we arrived at our destination, we usually walked from where we parked the car to our hunting area.

Those times are some of the best memories that I have. My brother and I hunted in some of the most beautiful woods in this country. The oak trees seemed to climb to the heavens. They were so huge that it was hard to see all the way to the top. It was not unusual for our squirrel dog, usually borrowed from our uncle or a good football fan, to tree four or five squirrels in one of those large oaks. Devone hit more squirrels than I did because I was not a very good shot. Like Jerry Clower would say, I just enjoyed shooting up there "amongst" them. I shot at ducks the same way.

What was so interesting about squirrel hunting was that when we found several squirrels in a tree and someone fired his gun, all the squirrels would disappear. Daddy would have us sit and wait and, usually within a few minutes, someone would spot movement and the firing would commence again. It was exciting to look up and down the tree and survey each limb to find that hairy critter. Those squirrels could hunker down on a limb so flat that you could easily overlook them. The only thing that gave them away would be a breeze that moved the hair on their tails.

The hunt was always a thrilling occasion, but what was more important was the time that we spent with our daddy and the things that we talked about while walking through the woods or waiting on those squirrels. Since our two younger brothers, Joe Beck and Andy, were only four and two years old when our daddy passed away, Devone and I tried our best to take them hunting as much as we could when they got old enough. I am sure that Joe Beck and Andy have the same wonderful memories about time spent in the woods, whether it was with their brothers or later with their own sons.

Once while I was in college, I received a lesson in economics while hunting with a man who went to our church. He took me squirrel hunting one afternoon. Just before going into the woods, he said to me, "When I go into the woods, I don't stop making money. I want you to learn to do the same. Here is $50. You made money while hunting today, and I don't want you to ever forget it." And I never did.

I am not a big hunter anymore, but I still go to the woods for a long walk or to sit in a deer stand and watch the wildlife. I still cherish the time.

Remembering Sam Hanna

My wife and I had just returned from a short visit with our daughter, who lives out of town. After completing my unpacking chores, I went to my computer to catch up on the e-mail news. One item of news caused a sinking feeling in my stomach: Sam Hanna, Sr., had passed away only several hours earlier.

I first heard of Sam Hanna when I was in the fifth grade. We had moved to Monroe, where my father had become the head football coach at Northeast Louisiana State College. Over the next several years, there was a name that I would become accustomed to hearing: Sam Hanna. Now I doubt that I was reading the editorials of the *Monroe Morning World* or the *Monroe Newsstar* at eleven years of age. Therefore, if I recognized the name of Sam Hanna, I heard it from my dad.

I am sure that my dad looked quite favorably upon Franklin Parish natives. He was a native of Franklin Parish also. Since my father was not the kind of man who believed in saying negative things about people, if I recognized the name of Sam Hanna at an early age, my father must have been saying some good things about him. My father always had a deep respect for those who did their job well. For that reason, I have either heard of or known of Sam Hanna, Sr., for almost fifty years.

Over the past four or five years, I got to know Sam Hanna, Sr., on a more personal basis. The Hanna family had been kind enough to allow me to write a column in the *Ouachita Citizen*. What I quickly learned from Sam was that he seemed to appreciate the columns that were personal and more of a human interest story. On several occasions, he would call or drop me a note to tell me that he thought the column was good and had enjoyed it very much. Wow! A compliment coming from one of the most respected newspapermen in the country, a true journalist, made me want to dig deeper into the emotions of the heart. I soon discovered that Sam appreciated the columns about family, father and child relationships, or hunting and nature.

On my last hospital visit, as soon as I had walked into the room and even though he was very sick, he complimented my writing. Can you believe that? As soon as he saw me, a man as sick as he was and barely able to talk said, "I enjoyed your column today." I was so humbled by his remark. An icon in the newspaper business offered praise for my column when I would have thought that it was the last thing on his mind.

On one earlier visit during a previous hospital stay, Sam shared with me about his quail hunts when he was a boy. He told me that he and his son, Sammy, Jr., had hunted in the same location years later. When he expressed to me how the quail population has almost been depleted, I could feel a true sadness from the heart of an outdoorsman.

He also told me with a slight sparkle in his eyes that he had played in the band at LSU. I wished that we could have visited much longer, but when he began to cough, I knew that our conversation needed to end. I enjoyed listening to and learning from someone who had had so many life experiences.

I am so glad to have known Sam Hanna. And Sam, like many people, I loved reading your column.

Holocaust Faith

Last week I wrote about prayer. This morning I was praying a prayer of healing. While I was praying, I saw an image of Jesus. It did not stay long, but long enough that I felt a feeling of encouragement and hope. Just that momentary figure of Jesus gave me a minute to grasp the security provided by His very presence. He was there for me. There was no lightning, thunder, or words—just Jesus.

For that brief moment, I clung to that image, because for the past several months my faith had been tried even to the point of giving up on the very foundation on which my faith has been formed over the years. Have you ever been to that point? Have you ever wondered if your beliefs could have been misguided? I have never thought that Jesus was not there for me. However, I have experienced times when I did question my own ability or inability to ask, seek, and find. I have found that it has never been too difficult to believe and have the faith of Paul when my family and I have been the recipients of glowing reviews. When all is well, all is well.

Several times this week, I was reminded of the Holocaust. I can't even imagine the atrocities these people faced. They lived in the very pit of hell every day and saw mankind at its very worst. I shiver to think about how far my faith would have carried me. How long would it have taken for me to turn against God? Oh, readers, most of us have never had our faith tried like the Jewish people did during the Holocaust.

I do not enjoy my own trials. They hurt. They anger me. But then I think of the intensity of the Holocaust. I learned a long time ago to never compare my trials with the trials of others. There is not one healthy thing about comparing. During a very trying time years ago, I started out by using the overused statement: "Look around and you will find someone worse off than you are." That worked for awhile, but as my experience seemed to grow worse, I would think of that statement again and answer, "I don't care."

I mentioned the Holocaust, not to compare (because comparing never works), but only to question the strength of my own faith. I will admit that my

> *"Some things have to be believed to be seen."*
> Ralph Hodgson

faith would have failed, and probably quickly. However, there is a verse in the Bible that strengthens my resolve to continue on this Christian journey: Now faith is the substance of things hoped for, the evidence of things not seen (Heb. 11:1, KJ21). I pray for the day that I walk not by my faith, but by the faith created by Jesus, who is the author and finisher (perfecter) of faith. I look forward to the day that I can walk by the faith that is a gift from God.

There have been two times in my life that I have experienced this type of faith. I miss it.

Football Games and a Honeymoon

My wife and I did not get to go too far on our honeymoon. We were married on September 22, and I was playing in a football game on the twenty-third. I was playing for the old Twin City Panthers, the first semi-pro football team in the Monroe and West Monroe area.

Donna, my new bride, sat with my mother and two younger brothers at the game. After one of the plays, Andy, my youngest brother who was quite young at the time, remarked to Donna that I was still lying on the ground. I had released out of the backfield to become a safety valve receiver. Our quarterback had thrown the ball a little high, and I had had to jump for it. I had made the catch, but the first thing that had hit the ground was my back. The second thing that had landed was a 250-pound linebacker, who came to rest on my rib cage. I felt as if someone had shot me with a 30-06 rifle. The pain was horrific.

While all of this was going on, Joe Beck, the next to the youngest, mentioned to my mother that Donna must be cold because she was shaking really badly. However, the weather was mild; she was shaking, not from the weather of course, but from not knowing the fate of her brand new husband.

The ambulance came out on the field, and I do believe that the three stooges were the attendants. It took them quite some time to figure out how to get the gurney to stay open. Once this problem was solved, I was loaded up, and we headed out with sirens blaring for the St. Francis Hospital. I could hear the three stooges discussing how to get to the hospital.

"How do we get to the hospital from here?"

One of them answered, "I don't know, but we just missed the street we should have turned on. We have to make the block and go back."

I could have sworn I heard the names Larry and Moe mentioned.

It turned out that I had torn some ligaments off my rib cage. Although I did not have to spend the night in the hospital, I did take home a bottle of pain medication to go along with the big shot they gave me in the emergency room. Donna and I returned to our apartment about four o'clock in the morning. Nice way to spend your honeymoon, huh, ladies? Now if you have never experienced tearing something away from your rib cage, then you have missed a good opportunity to enjoy a lot of pain every time you sneezed during the next month.

But this is not the end of the story. After being out for about a month, I received a call from our coach, who wanted me to bring my bag with my uniform and equipment to the next game, just in case I was needed. We were to play Texarkana for sole position of first place.

Well, about the middle of the second quarter, I was needed. I hurriedly put on my uniform and made my entrance with a hero's welcome. I stayed in the game long enough to run over a defender. When he tackled me, I knocked him out cold. Oh yeah, I forgot to mention that I did not get up either. So much for the Big S under my uniform.

How many people remember the Twin City Panthers? Some of the players were Pat Anderson, Tommy Gist, Moose Parrah, Eugene Hughes, Roy Shellings, "Bullet" Sims, Charles Smith, "Bear"McHenry, and me. We did not make much money, but we had a lot of fun.

"Honor Thy Father"
(A Father's Day Article)

Several years ago, a father shared an experience with me that he had had with one of his children. He said that he had been reading the newspaper while relaxing in his big La-Z-Boy when he felt someone looking at him. You know that strong feeling you get when someone is not only looking at you, but also thinking very strongly about you? As soon as he had lowered the newspaper, he saw those big brown eyes of his little five-year-old daughter looking into the eyes of her most adored man in the world. He said he could tell that his little daughter wanted to tell him something. He asked her, "Honey, do you need to say something to Daddy?"

With a sparkle in her eyes that made her words carry an impact that got this daddy's undivided attention, she said, "Daddy, I will be like you."

He said that he could not pick her up fast enough to give her a big hug. He told me that he knew the responsibility he had as a father, but when he heard these words coming from her, his awareness of this awesome responsibility was reinforced. This thought almost overwhelmed him.

"Honor thy mother and thy father" is one of the Ten Commandments. And since Sunday is Father's Day, I thought it would be a good idea to allow some sons and daughters a chance to honor their fathers:

"My father told me to approach life with a sense of humor and that the meaning of life is found in relationships—with God, others, and self."

"My daddy taught me to talk about the sins of others only when on my knees."

One lady said that her father told her that it's not what

other people do, how much money they save, or how much they give you. It's not how they look or what they say. It's how they make you feel.

"I learned compassion for everyone from my dad, who never met a stranger."

"My Father lives with sincere integrity, gracious humility, and quiet strength. I continue to strive to become like Him. What you are is what He is. What He is is what we wish all men could be."

"My dad, who was the most honest, loving, and kind man that I have ever known, taught me strength and determination to overcome adversity when faced with overwhelming life situations."

"Dad taught me that if I would work hard, I would make my own luck. He told me to always take care of the customers and the money will take care of itself. Always put in more than you take out. Take the road less traveled. Love your God. He said this with his performances and few words. We are still blessed to have him with us."

"My father said, 'Every person you meet knows something that you don't know. Always learn from them. You will begin to realize that the older we get, the more we realize how little we know.'"

"I learned to be fair to people and treat them as you would want to be treated. I learned to live a Christian life by watching him."

"My dad taught me the value of being determined, driven, and goal-oriented."

"Dad told me to always be faithful to Jesus Christ, our Lord and Savior. For, no matter what happens in this life, good and bad, He will always be there to bring us through it."

"My father taught me patience. It is the end result that matters."

HAPPY FATHER'S DAY!!!

How Old Is Too Old?

I can remember when a sportswriter came up to me after I had been out of coaching for a period of time. He told me that I had been a very good coach "in my day." That was the first time in my life that it dawned on me that I was getting older.

What is it about our country that does not respect age? It is a shame that we finally learn how to live but then are told that we "are too old." Now I am not completely over the hill, but I am "standing on top looking down."

Coach Bobby Bowden, head coach of Florida State, was the winningest coach in Division 1-A of the NCAA at the age of seventy-seven. Coach Joe Paterno, head coach of Penn State, is in his early eighties and is the second winningest coach. During the 2004 season, there was an outcry that Joe Paterno had gotten too old. People wanted to fire the "old man." In 2005, Penn State went 11-1. Now the naysayers have decided that maybe he is not too old. How ironic that the two winningest coaches in division 1A are two "old" guys.

Mary Kay Ash was forty-five when she began Mary Kay Cosmetics. Head coach of Grambling University Eddie Robinson, the winningest coach in college football, was seventy-six years old when he became the first coach to ever win 400 games on the collegiate level. Ronald Reagan was only twenty-one days away from turning seventy when he was a sworn in as the president of the United States. George Blanda played quarterback in the NFL until he was fifty years old. George Foreman won the heavy-weight championship again at the age of forty-five.

When are you too old? Never.

How to Think

I do wish that my preacher would have spent more time giving sermons on the effect of our thinking upon our lives. Unfortunately, I think that most preachers forty years ago were not aware of the power of words and thoughts. Even though the Bible tells us how we are to think and speak, not many preachers—with the exception of Norman Vincent Peale—spent much time on this subject.

However, this is my humble opinion about why things can change in our lives when things have been going on so well. It is so hard for us to move on after we have had some type of trauma in our lives or some negative experience that completely changes our thought processes. Nonetheless, if we have an experience that causes us to continue thinking about the negative impact of the experience, then I believe the Law of Attraction comes into place. As the Bible tells us, "As a man thinketh in his heart, so is he." The noted psychologist James Allen states that we become what we think about. Furthermore, I have heard many times that what we think about the longest becomes the strongest.

Philippians 4:7-8 says, "And the peace of God, which passeth all understanding, shall keep (guard) your hearts and minds through Christ Jesus. Finally, brethren, whatsoever things are true, whatsoever things are honest, whatsoever things are just, whatsoever things are pure, whatsoever things are lovely, whatsoever things are of good report; if there be any virtue, and if there be any praise, think on these things."

I Believe

One day, I was listening to the radio while traveling to go visit my daughter in Baton Rouge. I don't listen to much country and western because I am usually listening to an oldies but goodies station, but the country and western station was probably the only station that I could pick up in the hill country. A song that grabbed my heart strings began to play, and I knew that I had to have that song. As soon as I arrived at my daughter's, I asked her about the song and whether or not she had heard it. She said that she had. The song was "Believe" sung by Brooks and Dunn. We went to a store and bought the CD. I bought the CD, not only to listen to the music, but also to learn the words. The right words can change your life. I love songs and movies that inspire me and make me feel happy, alive, and healthy.

I listened to the CD for most of the way back to West Monroe, which was almost a four hour drive. I don't know that I have ever heard such a powerful song that moved me so deeply. I only wish that I knew how to sing. To be able to sing a song with so much meaning could add years to life. I thought that if any of the contestants on American Idol sang this song, they would win.

This song tells a story about a young boy and an old man named Mr. Wrigley. The boy's mother would send him over to the old man's house with food and gifts. The unlikely pair struck up a lasting friendship. They would sit out on the swing on Mr. Wrigley's front porch and talk.

During one of their visits, Mr. Wrigley told the boy that, when he was a young man, he had gone off to war. He told him that he had lost his wife and baby the same year. The young boy asked him, "How did you keep from going crazy?" The old gentleman answered him in a strange way. He told the boy that he was going to see them in awhile. Confused by the old man's answer, the young boy asked him how he could do that. The old man looked him straight in the eyes and replied, "I raise my hands, bow my head/ I'm finding more and more truth in the words written in red." He said these words from the Bible taught him how to believe.

Years later while the young man was off at college, Mr. Wrigley died. The young man spent some time reminiscing about the friend that had taught him so much during all of their visits. What he remembered more than anything was the day the old man looked him straight in the eyes and told him how to get through such hard times. "I raise my hands, bow my head/ I'm finding more and more truth in the words written in red./ . . . there's more to life than just what I can see." He had taught his young friend how to find answers to life.

I played this song over and over again all the way home, sometimes with tears rolling down my face. The words never got old. I thought back to the friendships that I had had in my lifetime. When I asked myself if I had ever had a "Mr. Wrigley" in my life, I realized that it was my Granddaddy Payne. What about you? Who was your Mr. Wrigley?

I Want to Know What Love Is

I once heard Lisa Marie Presley being interviewed. She was asked, "Where do the words to your songs come from?" She answered, "From the pain in my life."

One morning, shortly after one of my walks, I was watching a television program on which Wynonna Judd was being interviewed. After the interview, she sang the song "I Want to Know What Love Is." I was so touched by this song that I purchased her new album that very morning and listened to it over and over. Many great songs, books, poems, memoirs, and movies are born from the depths of pain and suffering, and this song is no exception.

Wynonna has gone though some tough trials in her life. She and her mother had a tumultuous relationship. She went through bankruptcy. She battled weight problems. She struggled with any meaningful relationship. From this turmoil came the words and songs of her new album. Just as impressive as the songs were the words written on the back of the CD's album jacket. Included are Scripture references such as I Corinthians 13:13; Matthew 5:16, 6:25-34; and the "Sermon on the Mount" from Matthew 7:1-29.

The words to the song "I Want To Know What Love Is" are as follows:

I gotta take a little time
A little time to think things over
I better read between the lines
In case I need it when I'm older
This mountain I must climb
Feels like the world's upon my shoulders
Through the clouds I see love shine

It keeps me warm as life grows colder
In my life there's been heartache and pain
I don't know if I can face it again
I can't stop now I've traveled so far
To change this lonely life
I want to know what love is
I want you to show me
I want to feel what love is
I know you can show me
I'm gonna take a little time
A little time to look around me
I've got nowhere left to hide
It looks like love has finally found me
In my life there's been heartache and pain
I don't know if I can face it again
Can't stop now I've traveled so far
To change this lonely life

On the fourteenth of February, we celebrate a day for love. Millions of roses, cards, teddy bears, hearts, and boxes of candy are presented in the name of love. These exchanges symbolize the love for family, friends, and even pets, yet each day we hear the whole world crying out, "I want to know what love is!"

Isn't it a shame that we have taken Jesus' simple message of love and complicated it so that very few of us even understand it? The two greatest commandments tell us simply to love God with all of our hearts and to love our neighbors as we love ourselves. Instead, we have created such a web of complex and sometimes confusing doctrines that we reject the simplicity of Jesus Christ. When we have learned to master these two commandments, I think that we will have found the answer to Wynonna's song, "I Want to Know What Love Is."

Is It OK for Us to Dream?

I watched a movie starring Kevin Costner the other night. I do not know the name of the movie (*For Love of the Game*). Even though I only saw the last part, I saw enough to cause me to run down memory lane.

Being a fair athlete, I experienced the joy of the limelight, but only on a small scale—high school and then college. I do have good memories, but as I watched this movie, I remembered some of the more painful times I experienced as an athlete. Similarly, the professional baseball player in the movie struggles with age and an injury that compromises his ability. The movie led up to his final game—and what a game it was! Having accepted that age and injuries had finally caught up with him, he pitched a perfect game.

As I sat there on my couch, I wondered what it must be like to take part in athletics on such a large scale, participate in the pros, and perform in front of as many as a hundred thousand people on a regular basis in the largest cities in America. What would it be like to play in an All-Star Game, the World Series, or the Super Bowl?

I can only imagine what that must be like. I can remember struggling with injuries on the high school and collegiate levels. It seemed as if every time I was nearing some degree of success, I would face some type of injury. I was not the most talented person in the world, but I was better than I thought I was. My offensive backfield coach in college was the first coach that made me feel like a good athlete. Up until that point, I had just thought that whatever success I might have achieved was just luck. Not until I competed on a collegiate level did I have enough confidence to feel that I was good. I loved to play the game. I was not fast, but I never was caught from behind. I learned that there was a lot of difference between someone who was naturally fast and someone who had a burning desire to score.

I dreamed of playing professional football, even though there was only one coach who thought I could play on that level. Coach Jim Coates, my backfield coach in college, thought I could play with the best of them. So many times in life, we need that person who believes in us until we can learn to believe in ourselves.

When I was coaching in Farmerville, there was a young man who served as our trainer. No one could take care of a training room like him. He knew what he wanted, and he knew how he was going to get there. He had always dreamed of becoming an orthopedic surgeon. Dr. Richard Ballard's dream came true.

I read in the paper that Chuck Finley was inducted into the Louisiana Hall of Fame. I thought about how proud Chuck's mom and dad must be of his success. (But big Chuck always reminded me that he was proud of all his children.) Since Chuck had played professional baseball against the greats in the largest stadiums in the most major cities, I thought that Chuck had lived a career that most of the world only dreams about. However, when I thought more about it, I realized that Chuck had himself become one of the greats. Will Chuck have a chance at the Hall of Fame in Cooperstown? Wow! What must it be like to even think about being considered? But remember, that is the stuff that dreams are made of.

It Is Hard to Hide from All of the Fans

When you do something stupid in front of an entire stadium of people, it is mighty hard to disappear. I was the head coach at a Class AA school. The school was Class AA because the principal wanted to play up. That should have been a red flag, but we all want to be the head coach. Why should my opponents having a lot more players to pick from make any difference? Duuhh!!! Like I said, I was young and I wanted to be a head coach.

One night, I was trying to get a particular play called. I must have sent in at least three different players on three successive plays, and I still could not get the right play into the game. One time, instead of one player coming out, I had two players come out. When the two players reached the sideline, I grabbed both of them by the jerseys and pulled them toward me so that they could hear my voice, which was already loud enough to be heard in the next parish. I guess that these two players saw something in my eyes that must have motivated each of them to come quickly. As I pulled each of them to me, they sort of wilted. Their helmets came together, and they looked like two mountain goats butting horns. You could hear the crashing sound of the helmets as they hit each other head-on. I was hoping that everyone else was watching the game and that no one saw this crazy coach make these kids head butt each other. Unfortunately, as always, there is that one fan that has had too much to drink and makes sure the incident is brought to everyone's attention. "That's it, coach! If they can't get it right, knock their heads together!"

144

On another occasion, I was making the half-time adjustments to the team's attitude. I was going to pick out one of the tougher players to use for an example in order to motivate the rest of the team. I knew that if they saw me correcting one of the better players, the rest of them would certainly feel that they were next. As I reached over to get the player from off of the bench, I grabbed his jersey to help expedite his movement. However, my hand slipped from his jersey and hit him in the mouth. Of course, I bloodied his lip. Now, although I did not mean to break his lip, I think the other players took it as a warning. "My goodness. If Coach Payne will do that to our star, what will he do to the rest of us?"

As I matured as a coach, I thought that maybe Coach Bill Ruple's psychology was much safer and much saner. For instance, when I was a junior at Neville, we were ranked number one in the state, but we were being beaten by Baker High 20 to 0 at half-time. We expected Ruple to come charging through the door, throwing a tantrum, but the coaches did not even show up at half-time. A few minutes before we were to go back out for the second half, Ruple opened the door and said, "You boys are shook. Just relax. Now go back out and play like you are supposed to." We went out and scored fifty-three points in the second half. Baker scored zero. I think Ruple had it right. Maybe that is why Coach Ruple was a legend and I sold insurance.

The Moment of Critical Mass

I watch motivational videos from a website called simple truths.com. These videos make me feel as if I am faster than a speeding bullet, more powerful than a locomotive, and able to leap over a tall building. Of course, I am exaggerating, but it does make me feel like Superman. It raises my expectations and increases my desire to achieve.

One of the videos is called *212°*. Water at a temperature of 211° is hot. When the water gets to 212°, it boils. When it boils, it makes steam, which can power a locomotive. That one extra degree makes all the difference in the world. It is the little things. That one degree of extra effort separates the ordinary from the extraordinary, the common from the uncommon, and the good from the great.

The New York Giants based their motivation upon "winning the Super Bowl." Their purpose was securely fastened to the Super Bowl—one game only. The New England Patriots' motivation was to break a record. New York was playing for their lives.

> *"Never save something for a special occasion. Everyday in your life is a special occasion."*
> Author Unknown

New England was playing to remain undefeated. It was that one degree of difference in their motives that gave New York the edge.

The difference in winning first place and second place in the Indy 500 is over $600,000. The margin of victory over the past ten years in the Indy 500 is 1.52 seconds. The difference in 1.52 seconds is $400,000 per second. It is the little things that make the great big difference.

If you begin with only a penny and double your money every day, your investment after thirty days results in a savings of $10,737,418.23. Stop saving at twenty-nine days, and you will lose over $5,000,000.

Social scientists point out that it is the little things that begin to add up. Once the little things reach a certain point, the momentum for change becomes unstoppable. This moment is called the moment of critical mass—the moment when the little things make a great big difference. This moment is the boiling point, when the unstoppable critical mass becomes as powerful as a locomotive.

Never forget the power that is in little things.

It Takes a Long Time

I have always told folks that it is always painful when we lose a parent, no matter how old or young we are or how old or young our parents are. I can remember my father's funeral as if it were yesterday. Reality concerning the Payne family could not have been more pronounced than it was when our preacher brought a copy of the newspaper to church. All the way across the front page of the News-star, with a huge picture underneath, were the words "Coach Devone Payne, Age 44, Dies." Now we all like to see our father's name in the paper, but never under such traumatic circumstances. As a young teenager, I had thought that somehow I was going to figure out a way to reverse this horror story. But there it was in black and white. The nightmare was real, and it was only the beginning of what would become a fifty year learning experience.

I can remember them opening up the Sunday school rooms at College Place Baptist Church before Daddy's funeral because the sanctuary had filled to capacity. They relayed the sound to all these rooms so that people could at least hear what was being said. One thing that stood out was the Northeast choir in their bright, shiny maroon and gold robes. I don't think that the Mormon Tabernacle Choir could have performed any better. I remember the large number of college students that were in attendance. I can remember seeing a lot of my classmates and members of my football team.

My two younger brothers were too young to attend their own father's funeral. They stayed at the house with Jettie.

Jettie Washington had been a part of our family for years. She began working for us when Daddy became the head football coach at Tallulah High School. Even though we had been gone from Tallulah for quite some time, she was the one who was called to come keep Joe Beck and Andy.

I remember so vividly the length of the funeral procession. Daddy was to be buried in the Masonic Cemetery in Crowville, his hometown. First, the Monroe police took care of the city limits. Then the Ouachita Parish Sheriff Department led the procession until the Franklin Parish Sheriff Department took over at the parish lines. We were told that the line stretched for miles. The graveside service was delayed until all the cars had arrived.

Even though I was only thirteen, I knew by the showing of the large number of people at the church and the fact that most of them drive another forty miles in the funeral procession to go to the graveside services that I had a special father who was a special man to many people. Now, almost fifty years later, I am reminded almost on a daily basis of how lucky I was to have had Coach Devone Payne for a daddy for those thirteen short years.

I shiver when I think what would have happened to me over the years without special people in my life. A strong thirty-seven-year-old widow was the key. She never wavered in her new roles as father, provider, encourager, and disciplinarian. My football coaches became my surrogate fathers who took care of me away from home. Coaches Van Leigh, Bill Ruple, Charlie Brown, Chick Childress, and Jim Coates were much more than coaches. Although I was very fortunate to have these people stand in the gap for me for so many years, I will never know anyone quite like my father. I am sixty-six years old, and I still miss him.

It Takes Only One Idea

The other day as I was walking through the Brookshire's parking lot to go to the grocery store, I looked at all the businesses there in the shopping center. I felt a slight rush as I commented to myself mentally, "Every one of these businesses was started by one man's or one woman's idea." All that I could observe while walking across the parking lot was begun with one idea—asphalt, cars, windows, paint, tires, plastic, electricity, signs on the buildings, pizza, aluminum, and glass. The next time you are riding down the road, take a look around you and note that everything you see was first a thought.

Many inventions or creations came from someone solving a problem. The next time you catch yourself complaining, ask yourself, "What could I create or invent that would make this better?" From this one question, businesses were born and products were invented. Problems are only markets in search of solutions.

A drink in Pittsburgh had its name changed to root beer because the people of a tough mill town would not drink an herb tea. Ray Kroc built McDonald's, one of the world's most recognized franchises, based upon the idea that families needed an attractive atmosphere when out to eat—especially one that provided clean rest rooms. During World War II, due to the gasoline shortage, Soichiro Honda attached a motor to a bicycle in order to go get food for his family. The Hondo Motor Company was born out of the desperate situations that this war created. Steven Jobs and Steven Wozniak saw a market for personal computers before the big boys (corporations) had even given it a thought. This idea was generated when the two of them were members of the Homebrew Computer Club, a place where high school students were given an opportunity to share their ideas about computers.

This club reminded me of the club I formed for students when I was teaching. The club's name was PACE—Positive Attitude Changes Everything. The students met in my classroom on Mondays at 7:30 in the morning. I wanted a place where students were encouraged to think and where they had the opportunity to share ideas about setting and reaching goals. I stressed to them that it took only one good idea to change their lives or the lives of others. Ewing Kauffman, the founder of Marion Laboratories, always reminded others that you can't stop a man who thinks.

When I read stories about people such as Joshua Lionel Cowen, who invented the "electric flowerpot," my desire to motivate students only increases. Cowen sold the rights to his "electric flowerpot" to Conrad Hubert. Since Hubert had absolutely no success selling this invention, he detached the illuminatory parts and began to sell them separately. In other words, he found a solution to his problem, which became the Everyready flashlight. Oh, by the way, Lionel Cowen was the inventor of the Lionel electric trains.

I am sixty-six years old, and I still get excited when I think about sharing stories with students about men and women who changed their own lives and the lives of others with one good idea. I always wanted my students to know that they, too, could be one of these men or women, and I might add that you can too. Two exciting books you can read to help you launch your ideas are *Entrepreneurial Megabucks*, by David Silver, and *Entrepreneurs*, by Joseph and Suzy Fucini.

Jack of All Trades, Master of None

Whoever made the statement, "Jack of all trades and master of none," evidently had never met Benjamin Franklin, Thomas Jefferson, or Richard Branson. "Jack of all trades and master of none" was usually a negative feature of an individual who tried many things but did not achieve success in any area. Also, whoever was responsible for this quote had never heard of a polymath or a Renaissance man. (A polymath is an individual who is very knowledgeable and gifted in many areas.) I have spent the past several hours researching some men who would be considered polymath or Renaissance men.

Ben Franklin was a printer, author, inventor, philosopher, politician, diplomat, Freemason, scientist, inventor, and great statesman. Among his inventions were the Ben Franklin stove, the lightning rod, odometer, and bifocal glasses. Furthermore, he founded the first public library, served as a postmaster, and started the first fire insurance company. He was instrumental in the drafting of the Declaration of Independence and was one of its original signers. Because he established the Philadelphia Academy that later became the University of Pennsylvania, he had a great impact on the educational system. He was the author of *The Way to Wealth, What's the Big Idea?, Poor Richard's Almanac, Ben Franklin's Rules of Management,* and *The Autobiography of Benjamin Franklin,* which he did not complete before his death. As early as 1790, he urged the abolition of slavery, becoming one of the first men to do so. Finally, he was considered one of America's greatest statesmen and diplomats.

Thomas Jefferson was a jurist, diplomat, writer, inventor, philosopher, architect, horticulturist, archeologist, paleontologist, and one of the main authors of the Declaration of Independence. Furthermore, he was the father of the University of Virginia, the governor of Virginia, and the third president of the United States of America. Being also a prolific inventor, he invented the mould plow, wheel cipher, sundial, Great clock, and a type of bookstand. He also perfected the polygraph and created revolving chairs. President John F. Kennedy said to a group of Nobel Prize winners who had gathered at the White House, "With this gathering of this group of Nobel Prize winners, this is the greatest gathering of knowledge that has ever been assembled in the White House—with the exception of Thomas Jefferson when he dined alone."

Although he does not have a corporate headquarters, Richard Branson is one of the most colorful, interesting, irreverent, and positive people on this planet. He started with a mail order business, a magazine (*Student*), and a record shop. The record shop became his bell cow that he sold for one billion dollars. He sold Virgin Music in order to have the cash to boost his new airline, Virgin Airlines. From this beginning, Richard Branson has developed the Virgin brand for over 150 companies. Every business comes under the name "Virgin Group." Included under the Virgin Group are air and rail travel services, telecommunications, financial services, retail, hotels and leisure, music, drinks, and web-based media.

Branson always has controlling interest anywhere from 51 percent to 100 percent of the ownership of each company. His number one mission in each company is to develop a brand that is highly recognized for marketing purposes. This concept of developing names into brand names has been used successfully by Michael Jordan, Nike, Hannah Montana, Britney Spears—who wrecked her marketability, Donald Trump, and many others. Although Richard Branson did not use his name, he developed the Virgin label second to none.

The Wisdom of Proverbs

Someone suggested that I should read one chapter of Proverbs every day. He emphasized that I make sure to not read more than one chapter each day. I can read the chapter as many times as I would like, but I cannot jump ahead to the next chapter. If there are less than thirty-one days in the month, I can make up the difference. I have been doing this since the first of the year.

I have been a regular reader of my Bible since the third or fourth grade. All of us who were raised Baptist remember that we had to read the Bible daily in order to make a hundred for the week on our giving card. Some of us created the habit of reading our Bibles during these times. Even though I am not a big doctrine man and probably not 100 percent Baptist (whatever that means), I formed some wonderful habits that paid off because of the training I received from my Baptist upbringing. Some of my other-than-Baptist habits used to scare my devoted Baptist mother. Since we read the Bible as a family every morning before we headed out to school, my Bible reading came from family as much as my church.

Sometimes I ought to be ashamed of myself for not showing more on the application side of my training. I have a very dear friend who coached with me for several years. Our families became close, and we have remained close ever since. This friend is an amazing person. I should be the one with the great faith because I have gone to church much more than he has, but my faith does not touch his faith. I have not found many people with the type of faith he has shown throughout his life.

He and his wife split up many years ago. The divorce caused many problems for their kids. One of the children had major problems. My [essay] is not long enough to list all of the problems and challenges this boy went through since the divorce. I have never seen a man stick with his child like my friend did through jail time, drugs, arrests, DWIs, car wrecks, expulsions from school, and so on. Most of us probably would have given up. However, I watched this daddy's unshakable faith see the son through it all. After many, many years of highs and lows, peaks and valleys, the light in this son's life has begun to shine because his father never gave up his belief that God was seeing him through.

Here I am the big church-goer. I was supposed to be the example of a faithful follower of Jesus Christ, yet it was a true friend, and true believer, who has shown Donna and me what a faithful father is.

Jesus' Temptations

Do we believe what the Bible says? I have come to a place in my life where I realized I must trust fully that the Word of God is literally true. Why shouldn't I? The Bible says that God cannot lie. Numbers 23:19 — "God is not a man, that he should lie . . . hath he said, and he not do it? Or hath he spoken, and shall he not make it good?" Titus 1:2 — "In hope of eternal life, which God, that cannot lie. . . " Joshua 21:45 — "Not a word failed of any good thing which the Lord had spoken. . . . All came to pass." Hebrews 10:23 — "Let us hold fast our confession of our hope (faith), without wavering, for He who promised is faithful."

I have found that the confession of scripture is one of the strongest forms of prayer. When I am awakened at night by worries, I am assured that I am answering these nightly disturbances with God's Word. Why should we learn to pray God's Word? Ephesians 6:10-13 tells us that we are not wrestling against flesh and blood. Since our battle is spiritual, not physical, we must put on the whole armor of God; 2 Corinthians 10:4-5 tells us how to fight and what to fight with. "For the weapons of our warfare are not carnal, but mighty through God to the pulling down of strongholds." What kind of strongholds? Illnesses, financial worries, marital challenges, family concerns, un-forgiveness, bitterness, anger, fear—these strongholds control our thoughts, thus controlling our actions and reactions to life.

When I was reading Luke 4:1-13 concerning Jesus' temptations in the wilderness, I saw what Jesus used as the weapon to withstand Satan's temptations and was given confidence that responding to life's problems by confessing the scriptures is right on target. Jesus answered Satan every time by saying, "It is written." Every temptation was overcome by quoting scripture. If it is good enough for Jesus, it is certainly good enough for me.

Life Lessons

For many years, I have been writing down quotes, statements, and power phrases, recording them in 4x6 spiral-ruled index cards. I have filled twenty-five of those fifty-page index cards, which adds up to 1,250 quotes. I would like to share some of these quotes with you. It is amazing what an impact a few words can make. Many of these statements I wrote myself, and I call them my life's lessons. I have learned a few things in life, but my trouble has been the successful application of this knowledge.

1. Regrets are yesterday. Anxiety is tomorrow. The present is the only place to be healthy. —*RCP*
2. Why do we Christians have so many stress-related disorders if we believe our faith? —*RCP*
3. The #1 healer—"LET GO!" —*RCP*
4. Leaders are called to live by a higher set of standards, and those leaders go by the names of Mother and Father.
5. Losing is not fun, but if you have never lost, you have never won. —*RCP*
6. He who angers you contains you—the reason for forgiveness.
7. Respect is something that takes a whole lifetime to gain, but only a few seconds to lose. —*RCP*
8. A true friend is someone who reaches for your hand and touches your heart.
9. Have you heard the saying that you learn through all your mistakes, pain, and suffering? I have decided that I would rather remain ignorant. —*RCP*
10. Be who you are and say what you feel, because those who mind don't matter and those who matter don't mind.

Living Up to a Name

Living up to a name while growing up can become a stepping stone or a stumbling block. If you know what it feels like to be compared to someone every day of your life, then you can identify with this remark: "Son, if you are half the man your father was, you are a pretty good man." What a wonderful feeling to know that your father was so highly respected! However, for those of you that know what it is like to be compared to someone before you who has done well, you know that living up to that person can become a heavy load. Sons who had a father with a good name, daughters who had a mother who was an achiever, and brothers and sisters who were always compared to an older sibling know the pressures of living in the shadows.

I remember the night I finally realized that I had made a name of my own. I was the head football coach at Farmerville High School. We were to play the Tallulah Trojans in that same stadium where Devone Payne's Trojans had become legendary. I was bringing a team that was a four-touchdown underdog, but my players could feel something special about to happen. We sat in a group on the field hours before the game, and I talked to them about my father and about what had happened on this exact field. I remember saying to them before we got up to go get dressed for the game, "Just don't embarrass me."

I have never seen a group of fifteen and sixteen-year-olds play as if they were on a mission. They had a job

> *Life is an echo. What you send out comes back.*
> Chinese Proverb

to do. They knew how important this game was for "their" Coach Payne. I never told them how important it was to me. They just knew it.

With only a few minutes into the first quarter, the Farmerville Big Orange, the Farmerville Farmers had already scored twenty-one points. I could not relax until the game was over. No, this was not for the state championship or even a district championship; these kids were playing for something much bigger. Something mysterious—even majestic—fell over that stadium that night. Something that seemed larger than life. Those young men handed their coach not only a 27 to 6 victory, but also a defining moment in his life.

After the game, a lady from Tallulah came running up to me and said, "Robert Charles, I watched your daddy's teams play for years, and I thought he was the best; but after watching your team tonight, I believe you are even better." Wow! I had finally arrived. I was now Robert Charles Payne.

Of course, I had not become better than my father—I did not want to be. However, I had discovered on that cool autumn night that I did not have to be in my father's shadows. I had never been in his shadows, because soon after I was born, he let me stand on his shoulders so I would able to see much farther down the road than he ever could. Our shadows had always been connected, and because of him, my shadow had always been the one on top.

For those of you who have felt the pressure of living up to someone, always remember that our fathers, our mothers, our sisters, and our brothers are who they are. They are the best at who they are, but you are the best at who you are. And that is what's important.

Lukewarm

If Christians ever need to be Christian, it had better be now. I don't mean lukewarm. Remember that lukewarm Christians were the ones God spewed out of His mouth.

Have you thought about how much the world has changed since we were young? How much have the movies changed? How much has television changed? At one time, you would not even hear the word "darn." Last night during family prime time, I heard almost the ugliest words you could hear before I could even find the remote. My granddaughter was sitting on the couch with me. The show had been okay up to that moment. The only word I did not hear was the "f" word. The show was even on one of our main channels.

Violence, torture, grisly images, language, sexual material, and drug use—these are just a few of the terms that describe the movies that are playing. What is really disturbing is that these changes took place during our watch. I heard a man once say that if everyone would sweep his own front porch, the entire city would be cleaned.

I am reading a book for the third time that has a formula for change. How many people does it take to change something? The book's formula was the square root of 1 percent of the population. There are over 300,000,000 people in the United States.

> "Motivation does not last, but bathing does not last either. That is why you must do it daily."
> Zig Ziglar

Using this formula, only 1,739 people are needed to change

the country. Only 1,739 people with a mission are needed to return America to its Christian principles—not our Christian principles, but the principles as presented in the Bible. Are there 1,739 people out there who want to live as Jesus would have us live? The way the world is going, I do believe we may see the day when we will have to make a choice—a clear choice.

Mentors

One night this week while I was at my computer, thoughts of my former coaches came across the screens of my mind. I thought about what I had learned from each of them—not only from those who coached me, but also from those I coached under as an assistant.

Van Leigh was the first coach I served under. I was his assistant at Lee Junior High. If you did not believe in discipline, you could not coach with Van Leigh. He prepared his players for their high school years. Coach Leigh was extremely loyal to Neville High School.

I had accepted an assistant coaching job under Tommy Bankston at Winnfield Senior High School, but while Donna and I were actually moving to Winnfield, Tommy accepted the principal's job. I was disappointed when I found out, but after having a good talk with Tommy, Donna and I decided to stick with our decision.

Tommy had played football for my father at Louisiana College in Pineville, Louisiana. Those who had played for my father always returned the favor by in turn teaching me. I learned so much about leadership from Tommy Bankston. I don't know if I have ever seen such a dynamic leader. He was definitely the commander-in-chief. Tommy was fearless with his decisions, and I saw him make some tough ones and never waver, even when the public did not agree.

I incorporated the three-step passing game that Tommy had used when he coached with my own passing game, and I would use this system for the remainder of my coaching career. My guess is that this three-step system probably was responsible for seven or eight thousand yards in passing, along with sixty or seventy touchdowns in a six-year period. Jerry Wheeler, the quarterback when I was the head coach at West Monroe, threw for well over a thousand yards and scored seventeen touchdowns in 1978.

I coached under Jim Bruning at Natchitoches-Central in Natchitoches, Louisiana. Jim had his own style, but there was never any doubt that he was in charge. He would never allow any of his assistants to be the recipients of any unkind criticism. After coaching with Jim for one year, he asked me if I wanted to take over as the head coach for the coming year. Although I wanted to be a head coach, I knew that Jim had a tremendous rapport with the black community. Since I had not been there long enough to build this kind of trust, I was satisfied to serve as Jim's assistant until my youngest brother, Andy, graduated. I was not aware of how much I had learned from Jim until I left to take the head coaching job at Farmerville.

When I was at Farmerville, I learned what a great advantage it was to have a big principal. My principal, Malvin Sistrunk, was big. He had fists about the size of a horse's hoof. One day, Malvin called me from his office to tell me to stay close because he had a parent coming up to the school to whip him and might need my help. After I hung up the phone, I realized that if Malvin needed my help, this parent must be a giant. I thought about leaving. I figured if there was anything he could not handle, I did not even need to be around. Later, I discovered that Malvin had been playing a joke on me. Nonetheless, it was an asset to have a big principal in case I ever needed help.

I would have to write a whole separate book to share what I learned from coaches Chick Childress, Charlie Brown, Bill Ruple, Jim Coates, and Coach Devone Payne, my father. Maybe one day I will do just that. I was extremely fortunate to have played under outstanding coaches and men like these. All of these men had a tremendous impact upon my life.

Mind Games

The other night, I received a phone call from my youngest son, Beck, who is a youth director at Family Church in West Monroe. He had just watched a girls' basketball game between Claiborne Christian School and Summerfield and told me that the game had been unbelievable. Claiborne had fallen behind 19-2 right off the bat. Many teams would fold when it looked as if they were getting ready to take a shellacking. This team is very young, with only one being a senior and the rest being much younger. You would expect such a young team to be devastated as they quickly fell behind seventeen points. However, as Paul Harvey would say, "Now for the rest of the story." The final score was as follows: Claiborne 5—Summerfield 52.

Have you ever wondered about games like this? What are the ingredients that motivate a team to come from such a deficit and still win the game? We know that teams don't suddenly get better or improve physically right before our eyes. No, the answer is not in the physical realm, but in the mental realm.

Mustard Seed

Have you ever asked God to increase your faith? Have you ever caught yourself saying, "I need more faith"?

I want to ask you this question: "Is it more faith that we need?" Let's look at Matthew 17:20 — "And Jesus said unto them, 'Because of your unbelief: for verily I say unto you, if ye have faith as a grain of mustard seed, ye shall say unto this mountain, remove hence to yonder place; and it shall remove; and nothing shall be impossible unto you.'" Did Jesus say to them that their faith had to be as big as a mountain? No! He said that if they had faith the size of a mustard seed, they could move mountains. Wow!

Jesus does not tell us that we have to have faith the size of a mountain. He says that if we have faith the size of a mustard seed, we can tell the mountain to be removed. Jesus is saying that it does not take much faith at all and that the key is to use the faith you have. It is not the amount of faith, but the application of faith. Faith is so powerful that if we have faith the size of a mustard seed, we can move mountains. Wow! Wow! Wow! How encouraging! Don't worry about growing your faith. Use what you have.

My Heroes

When we were growing up, we all had heroes. When I think back to when I was a boy, I remember that my heroes were Jesus Christ, my mother, and my daddy. I did not have any athletic or famous heroes. Today, I have more heroes than I did as a little boy. When I think of heroes, I think of the now deceased Howard Hicks of Farmerville. At the same time that I was the head football and baseball coach at Farmerville, Howard was the man who took care of washing, cleaning the dressing rooms, and attending to every little detail you could think of. When Howard was born, his umbilical chord cut off his blood supply, causing him to have many problems that physically limited him. It took me awhile to learn how to understand Howard, but after being around him for a little while, I could understand everything he said. I have never seen anyone take care of his job like Howard took care of his. Would I call Howard handicapped? No, I would not. For whatever his purpose was upon this earth, he met it 100 percent.

Another hero of mine is also deceased. His name was Milton Day. Milton was a bad diabetic. I had met him years before in a Christian men's organization. Over a period of three or four years, and because of half a dozen surgeries or more, I watched Milton lose both legs up to his thighs. Yet he could still smile and thank God for his life. I would never promise that I could do that. He would get depressed every now and then, but he always snapped out of it. When you walked into his hospital room, he would give you a big smile and say, "Praise God. Isn't life good?" Yes, Milton is a hero of mine.

Then there was my covenant partner Randy McLemore. We lost Randy five years ago. Randy and I met every day somewhere. We talked and prayed over the phone several times a day. Randy was a businessman who ran a multi-million dollar business, but his emphasis was on Jesus Christ. I never saw him put his business or his money before his Lord. I admired many of his attributes—family man, business savvy, financial expert, leader, and devoted Christian. I always thought Randy would have made a tremendous statesman. However, what I cherished the most was his loyal friendship.

I have another hero who was in my Life Group class at First West. Jerry Durham had needed a kidney transplant for quite awhile, but he had never let it stop him from enjoying life to its fullest. He and his wife Mary took long trips that they planned out in advance so that he could be medically attended to if need be. Jerry took dialysis at home or wherever he and Mary might be.

One morning at our prayer group, we almost lost Jerry due to a heart attack. I have to give the 911 folks and the ambulance service an A+. I could hear the siren before I hung up the phone. Jerry recovered fully, and he did not let this experience delay his zest for life for more than a day or two.

Jerry and Mary's presence in our class was always a great encouragement. I knew that Jerry did not feel good on some of those Sunday mornings, yet he and Mary were there. I was so honored to have visited with him, to have held him so he could sit up in his bed to ease the discomfort, and to have prayed with him only hours before he passed away.

I have always been an admirer of ordinary people who do extraordinary things.

A Daughter and Her Daddy

I know that some dads like to take their daughters hunting. I took Laurie, my daughter, deer hunting for the first time when she was about ten years old. Since she had shown an interest in going, we packed up the gear and headed for Union Parish. However, Laurie had no desire to shoot anything; she just wanted to go and see the deer. When we had been in our box stand for a little over five minutes, Laurie looked up at me and asked, "Where are the deer?" When she discovered that we might have to sit and wait a spell before seeing any deer, she decided that she was not a hunter.

What Laurie and I enjoyed doing together was track. When she was in junior high, I knew she was not fast enough to be a sprinter, but I thought she had enough speed to become a fairly good hurdler. Because of her small size, it was very difficult for her to three-step in between the hurdles. She had to learn the four-step technique.

One of the fondest memories that I have of Laurie and me was during her freshman year at West Monroe High School. She had qualified for regionals, and the meet was held in Lake Charles. When it came time for Laurie's race, I watched the runners get into their blocks. Because I was up in the stadium near the finish line, I could not see the starting line very well. I was trying to film the race, but my hands were shaking so badly that it looked like an earthquake was taking place. Yes, Dad was nervous. There are so many things that you have to get right when you are running the hurdles. It is a little bit like playing the piano. When you make a mistake, everyone knows it. When you hit a hurdle, everyone knows it. I saw the smoke come from the starter's gun. Then I saw another puff of smoke: someone had jumped. Since Laurie was already getting back into her blocks, it could not have been she who jumped. Next, I noticed the starter standing in her lane, and then I saw Laurie walk off the tracks. She was the runner who jumped.

My heart ached for her. It was a big meet for a freshman. I went down to meet her, and I saw those tears. Hugging her neck, I asked what happened. She told me that when she was in the starting position with her hips up ready to go, she began to lose her balance. To keep from falling, she moved her hand slightly to steady herself. The starter told her that this movement caused her to have a false start. She thanked him for telling her and got back into her blocks. He then told her that she was out of the race. She had no clue that she was eliminated because all of the meets up to that point had allowed two false starts.

What an experience to ride four hours to see my daughter false start. Her race was over in a millisecond. To try to lighten her disappointment, I told her that it was the fastest race I had ever seen. I would have ridden eight hours to watch my daughter false start. Her track coach let her ride home with me, and we spent four hours having the time of our lives all the way back to West Monroe.

That was only yesterday, and now she is already twenty-nine.

A Few Words Can Speak Volumes

Sometimes you can learn more from a few simple words that have meaning than you can from a litany of words that speak too much. I have collected over 1,000 of these statements over the years. Some have made me chuckle. Some have made me think of challenging times. However, all of them have made me think. I have shared a few of these statements below, giving credit to those who were responsible for making the statement but leaving it blank if the speaker is unknown.

1. The mind is the boss of the body.
2. If you find the job you love, you will never work another day of your life. —*Curtis Carlson*
3. What is essential is invisible to the eye.
4. You cannot plough a field by turning it over in your mind.
5. Faith is what makes stuff stuff.
6. You can't send a duck to eagle school.
7. You can't throw an egg in the barnyard and expect it to be crowing by morning. It takes time to get the job done. —*Cavett Robert*
8. Change is good. You go first.
9. The empires of the future are the empires of the mind. —*Sir Winston Churchill*
10. To build may take a long time, but to destroy can be the thoughtless act of a single moment. —*Sir Winston Churchill*
11. Never be afraid of dying, but never be afraid of living either. —*RCP*

12. The secret of happiness is not in doing what one likes, but in liking what one has to do. —*James E. Barrie*

13. Bad experiences can either beat you up or lift you up. —*RCP*

14. He that cannot forgive others breaks the bridge over which he must pass himself; for every man has a need to be forgiven. —*George Herbert*

15. During the Depression, there were no poor people jumping out the windows.

16. Sometimes I feel as God must feel—when I know that I am right about something, but nobody will listen. —*RCP*

17. Purpose—we become what we are committed to.

18. When you live in the past, you become history. —*RCP*

19. A man is not what he thinks he is; but what he thinks, he is. —*Max R. Hickerson*

20. If you drive illegally in the United States, they take your driver's license. If you are in the US illegally, they want to give you one.

21. Anger is only one letter short of danger.

22. You haven't taught until they have learned. —*John Wooden*

23. Health food nuts are going to feel funny when they are in the hospital dying of nothing. —*Red Foxx*

24. Growing old is mandatory. Growing up is optional.

25. If not now, when?

26. My job as a school teacher was to make the student aware of his gifts. —*RCP*

27. Some cause happiness wherever they go; others whenever they go. —*Oscar Wilde*

28. I am not a teacher, but I am an awakener. —*Robert Frost*

29. I don't approve of political jokes. I've seen too many elected.

30. A friend knows all about you but likes you anyway.

31. I don't know the key to success, but the key to failure is trying to please everybody. —*Bill Cosby*
32. Perpetual optimism is a force multiplier. —*Colin Powell*
33. Love will die of neglect just as a flower, tree, or bush.
34. Nobody on the face of this earth can make you feel inferior without your permission.

When I taught school, I always had a very positive sentence written on the board for the students to see when they entered the room. I changed it on a daily basis.

Baby Blues

I hope that this makes the cut-off. I am sure you have had those weeks where the faster you go, the "behinder" you get. I remember one of the big vacations my family took when I was about four or five. A coach's salary did not allow for big vacations, but that summer we headed to Colorado. I had never seen a mountain in my life, and I was so excited when the mountains came into view. However, after what seemed like an eternity, I finally told my family, "The closer we get, the behinder we go." Have you ever had that feeling? We finally did reach old Pike's Peak. I am sure the experience of going up Pike's Peak initiated my fear of heights.

When I took our poodle, Pierre, out to use the bathroom this afternoon, I noticed with absolute wonder the beauty of God's work. The sun was headed to bed. The colors of the sky were breath-taking. A light blue tinged with pink mixed with the warm white of the sun. The horizon was painted with late afternoon darkness. It was if God had taken His pen and outlined all of the shadows of the trees. So many memories are birthed when I view these scenes, no matter how many times I see the view. I hear the squealers headed for the roost or the footsteps of a deer walking through the dry leaves. Every now and then, there would be a pause when the deer sensed something was not right. After a few minutes of cautious waiting, the deer would continue toward his evening meal.

Earlier I had taken Gracen, our newest granddaughter, on a walk around the backyard. When we stopped to listen to the sounds of a redbird, I watched as her beautiful blue eyes focused upon the sounds. Then she would take a look into her granddaddy's eyes, as if to say, "What makes that sound?" I looked into those beautiful baby blues that only God could create and said, "Bird. Hear the bird." How many times have we missed the marvels of God, whether it be the sounds and sights of nature or an afternoon stroll with those who make all of life worthwhile? Be still and know.

The Biggest Shock of My Life

When I was young, I loved to hunt, especially around my Grandmother and Granddaddy Payne's farm. Since my daddy was extremely safety conscious about hunting, my older brother and I usually had to flip, or choose who would hunt in front of the house and who would go behind the house. The best hunting area was behind the house. It had the pond, fields, and big trees up and down the creek bed that led to the pond. Because I had lost the flip on this particular day, I was hunting in front of the house. The front area being mainly oak trees, squirrels were about the only game available. There were a few rabbits, but no doves. And there were no deer in this area around Grandmother and Granddaddy's.

I was slowly slipping through the woods, looking up as I walked to see if I could spot any movement in the trees. Since it was during the winter, I did not have to worry about looking down for any snakes. Wishing that I was hunting behind the house, I was not too involved in what I was doing. There had not been much action going on up to this point, but things were about to change.

All of a sudden, I felt like a cat that had stuck its paw in a wall socket. Have you ever seen the pictures in the cartoons of a cat being shocked and its hair pointing straight out all over its body? If anyone had been watching, I am sure he would have thought I looked like that old cat. I did not know what was happening. Although I could not explain it, something had a hold on me. I did not know what it was, but it would not let me go. Whatever it was had me wrapped in fear. I even thought that maybe I was being attacked by some strange creature from out of space. This was an occasion when probably only a few seconds passed, but I think I saw my young life pass right before my eyes.

If I could have seen what was attacking me, I would have shot it. However, my shotgun seemed to be attached to something. Somehow my reactions must have allowed me to lift my gun in an upward reflex motion. When I did, whatever had hold of me let go.

I still could not understand what had happened. I was shook. It was as though I had just been shocked, but how in the world had I experienced this jolt in the middle of the woods? There was no reason for me to have even thought about being shocked, because there was no cause for electricity to be in this area. While searching for the culprit, I noticed a wire about the height of my waist running across the woods.

This land in front of my grandparents' house belonged to the neighbors, but in those days, you could hunt just about anywhere you wanted. All you had to do was make sure that you respected the property and the livestock while you were hunting.

I finally realized that the neighbors had put up an electric wire to keep their cows in the woods. This was something they had never done before. Their cows usually grazed in a pasture on the other side of their house, but for some reason they had turned them loose in the woods. Because of that, I received the shock of my life.

Growing Up a Coach's Son

I cherish my childhood memories of growing up in Tallulah, Louisiana. It was fun being a son of the football coach—almost like living a fantasy. Of course, when your dad's teams won 90 percent of their games, went deep into the play-offs every year, and played for the state championship for four straight years, it certainly helped you have fond memories. The blue and gold of the Tallulah Trojans was the pride of this agricultural community. Friday night football games along with church on Sunday and Wednesday were events that were the life-blood of the social fabric of this close-knit town.

Being reared on a football field was not bad. Because several players had to work on the farm in the afternoons, many of the practices were held at night. Devone and I would eat supper, and then Momma would take us to the stadium. Since Momma was a teacher, she would bring her school work with her and sit in the stands while Devone and I played on the football field. We knew better than to get in the way of practice.

Before we started elementary school, we would ride with our daddy to take some of the players home after practice. Some lived way out in the country. Boy, I learned so much going to those country homes. A few of those families were poor, but they never failed to offer "Coach Payne" and his sons a bite to eat. Have you ever heard of a country mom who could not cook? Daddy was very good at getting close to his players' parents. He enjoyed every visit and so did we. Devone and I would visit with the family pets, which were mostly good ole hound dogs. However, it was not rare for some of the families to have a coon or two or even squirrels in cages. Now, to two young boys, that was better than a big city zoo.

Coming home at night was just as entertaining. Madison Parish was deer country, and we saw plenty of deer. I wish that I had some pictures of the huge bucks we saw on our way home.

All of those football games over a nine-year period are etched into many of my thoughts. I remember having my own football games in a little grassy area beside the stadium while the big Trojans were playing theirs. At the time, I did not know that I was playing with two future LSU football stars—Chapman Lee and Leonard "Pops" Neuman. Both Chapman and Leonard became doctors.

What has been remarkable is the bond that has remained even after fifty years between the Payne family and the townspeople, players, cheerleaders, and students. My brothers and our wives were invited to a reunion this past year that was held at the Atrium for the former Tallulah Trojans. Standing around and listening to the talk about Coach Payne and the Trojans was quite a heart-warming experience. I was so glad that our wives got to hear the comments about Coach Payne, because they never had the opportunity to meet him. They witnessed the admiration for our daddy and mother, and the influence they both had on this group of people. Not many comments were made about our daddy without the additional admiring remarks about our mother. Momma and Daddy were a team. Momma epitomizes the saying, "Behind every good man is a good woman."

Because my wife lived in Tallulah herself for two years, she understands why I have such good memories of the town. As the television commercial says, "It's all good!"

In the Still, Small Voice

I received an email the other day with the title "Whispers." I want to share it with you because it is so true. I want you to think about the times that God may have shown up in your life but you ignored His presence because He showed up in some unexpected way.

The man whispered, "God, speak to me," and a bird sang, but the man did not hear. So the man yelled, "God, speak to me," and the thunder rolled across the sky. But the man did not listen. The man looked around and said, "God, let me see You," and a star shined brightly. But the man did not see. The man shouted, "God, show me a miracle," and a life was born. But the man did not notice. So the man cried out in despair, "Touch me, God, and let me know You are here." Whereupon, God reached down and touched the man, but the man brushed the butterfly away and walked on. The man cried out, "God, I need your help." Matching today's technology, an email arrived, reaching out with good news and encouragement. But the man deleted it and continued crying out to God. Don't miss God because His answer was not packaged the way you had expected.

I have found God and His answers in the tune I am unknowingly humming, and then I recognize that the words to the song were His answer to my prayer. I have awakened from dreams in the night that were answers to my prayers. Only the other night did Jesus show up in my dream. He was walking toward me in His white robe, and there seemed to be a crowd surrounding Him. As He passed me, His hands were glowing in warm orange and yellow. His hands were huge, and they seemed to glow all the way to His elbows. Now I visualize Him laying those healing, warm hands on me. He is there.

How has He shown up in your life? Have you missed Him? Remember it's in the still, small voice.

Sayings from Life

I thought I would use some of the sayings I have collected over the years in this [essay], giving credit to those who were responsible for making the statement but leaving it blank if the speaker is unknown. There can be so much wisdom in one sentence.

1. Don't try to swim in the waves of all your problems. Use them to surf successfully.
2. Christianity should be a transformation, not a therapy for what hurts. —*RCP*
3. I have never seen a confident person who is dumb. —*RCP*
4. The lowest ebb is when the tide turns. —*Henry Wadsworth Longfellow*
5. Opportunities never cease ... the opportunity to be kind, the opportunity to hold another's hand, the opportunity to be honest, the opportunity to love, the opportunity to make a friend, and the opportunity to encourage another. —*RCP*
6. Enthusiasm without knowledge is like running in the dark. —*RCP*
7. Don't fall in love with your assets. —*Clark Williams,* Century Telephone
8. You are either seeking God or trying to escape from Him. —*Walter Russell*
9. The possibility of feeling peaceful is never dependent upon some external event or circumstance.
10. I still miss my man, but my aim is getting better.
11. Life is what happens when you are making other plans.
12. You cannot have a new beginning, but you can begin a new ending.
13. The sweet voice of a child shakes the universe. —*RCP*

14. The thoughts I think are my seeds. The words I speak are my fertilizer. The plants I grow are my life.
    —"The Garden" by *RCP*
15. If each one sweeps in front of his own door, the whole street is clean.

I sought treatment last week because of the encouragement from my family and friends. I solicit your prayers this week. I am to take a bone scan and a cat scan this week to make sure the cancer has not spread. When I see my name on the prayer list each week, I am always encouraged to know there is someone praying for me. Thank you so much.

It was Billy Graham who said, "Tears are microscopes from which to see life better."

Number One Threat to Our Health

We could make a case for cancer as being the number one threat to the health of mankind. Or we could say heart diseases or possibly diabetes. However, none of these threats are the answer. I believe that the number one threat to the health of men and women is unforgiveness. After searching for the definition of *unforgiveness* in Webster's dictionary, I discovered, to my dismay, that the word *unforgiveness* is not even listed in the dictionary. I searched the Oxford unabridged dictionary on the internet. *Unforgiveness* was not listed. I typed in unforgiveness into my computer's spell check. *Unforgiveness* was not listed.

After having given it some thought, it did make sense. Unforgiveness is such a black thought, a bitter emotion, that it needed to be omitted from our language. The closest word that I could find for *unforgiveness was forgiveness.* Forgiveness is the exact opposite, or the antonym, for "unforgiveness." Maybe this is God's lesson concerning unforgiveness. It is better for us to learn to omit it.

Now let me get back on track with the theme for this [essay]. What is the number threat to our health? What can ruin our health? It is the destructive emotion of unforgiveness. If you think you cannot forgive someone and not affect your mental and physical well-being, then I have some lake property that I want to sell you in the Sahara Desert. Forgiveness is an appropriate act for our own benefit, our family's benefit, or even our future family's benefit. This action should be a "no-brainer."

How many times have you heard someone or yourself say, "I will never forgive them for that." Thus, we plant the first seeds of bitterness that can grow ill feelings that can trigger negative emotions that can lead to health problems. The Bible gives a warning for such actions: "Lest any root of bitterness spring up to trouble you, and thereby many be defiled," (Heb. 12:15, KJ21). "Defiled" is such a cancerous word. Defile whom? Many. At the top of the list under defilement is our own family, our own children, and our own grandchildren.

When we fail to forgive, we are giving complete rule over our lives to the very people whom we feel have wounded us so deeply. Not only have they hurt us, but also are we giving them complete control over the remainder of our lives, an act which will continue to affect our children and our grandchildren unless forgiveness enters into our formula for living.

Some years ago, I finally realized that forgiveness was not for the other fellow. Forgiveness was for me. If we want to free ourselves from this self-imposed prison, we have no choice. We must learn to forgive. There is no doubt in my mind that some of the ill feelings that I have harbored over the years toward some people have definitely affected my health. Did you hear what I said? It has affected *my* health—not their health.

Several years ago, I was diagnosed with prostate cancer. One day as I was driving down the road by myself, I had a strong impression. I silently said, "God, I am tired of all these diseases. I am tired of this pain. I am tired of going to the doctor. I am tired of taking all this medicine. I want to get well." I am sure this profoundly strong thought that followed my complaints was from God. "Robert Charles, if you want to get well, then you have to forgive *everyone* you hold any strong feelings toward." The simplicity of His answer was immediately acknowledged. Now what will I do with His advice?

Our Tears Magnify Our Sight

When I was going to school at Northeast Louisiana State College, I drove a bus in the afternoons for the city school system. I picked up the children at Sherrouse Elementary. On one particular day, the children had received their school pictures. I was watching as the boys and girls lined up to get on the bus, and I saw them showing their pictures to each other. Then I noticed this one particular boy. He was holding his pictures up against his chest as if he were hiding them so no one else could see them, but no one was even coming up to this child. Even if he had felt like sharing his pictures, he did not have anyone to share them with. My heart was aching for this little boy.

Later on in the day when I arrived back home, I wrote these words about what I had just witnessed: "To look down upon a child. To see sadness and sorrow in his eyes. To see a broken heart within a dear little one. To see an expression of pain because he thinks he's something he's not. Not one bit of happiness can pass through my soul until I can see a smile come across his face, because he knows, that someone else knows, that he's not what he thinks he is."

I have always had a deep emotional attachment for people who don't quite meet society's standards. As I get older, I seem to be becoming a much more emotional person. I can't even watch the movies *Hoosiers* or *Rudy* without tears welling up in my eyes. There is something about suffering and pain that either softens you up or hardens you up. I don't think I could coach today, for I am much more cognizant of how my coaching decisions could affect a player in a negative way. Although I don't think I could handle that responsibility now, I do miss the opportunity to encourage and inspire young people to be the best they can be. I miss the opportunity to develop a good self-image in them and to give them confidence to achieve, no matter who they are, no matter where they are from, and no matter how tough are the circumstances that many of our young people face in today's society.

I think of the early immigrants in the 1800s and early 1900s that came to America to achieve no matter what circumstances they faced. All they wanted was an opportunity to live the American dream. I do hope that the American dream is not being pilfered by the social engineers who are weakening the entrepreneurial spirit of the men and women of this country by trying to make us all walk to the same drum beat. It is okay if we are not all the same.

My father was a football coach. He was known as a tough task master, but my mother told me one time that Daddy cried in the movie when the legendary coach of Notre Dame, Knute Rockne, was killed in an airplane crash. My daddy, the tough coach, had a heart of gold. He taught me to always recognize and encourage the people who hold their pictures close to their chests.